Progress in IS

"PROGRESS in IS" encompasses the various areas of Information Systems in theory and practice, presenting cutting-edge advances in the field. It is aimed especially at researchers, doctoral students, and advanced practitioners. The series features both research monographs that make substantial contributions to our state of knowledge and handbooks and other edited volumes, in which a team of experts is organized by one or more leading authorities to write individual chapters on various aspects of the topic. "PROGRESS in IS" is edited by a global team of leading IS experts. The editorial board expressly welcomes new members to this group. Individual volumes in this series are supported by a minimum of two members of the editorial board, and a code of conduct mandatory for all members of the board ensures the quality and cutting-edge nature of the titles published under this series.

More information about this series at http://www.springer.com/series/10440

Mikael Lind • Michalis Michaelides •
Robert Ward • Richard T. Watson

Editors

Maritime Informatics

Additional Perspectives and Applications

 Springer

Editors
Mikael Lind
Research Institutes of Sweden (RISE)
Chalmers University of Technology
Gothenburg, Sweden

Michalis Michaelides
Cyprus University of Technology
Limassol, Cyprus

Robert Ward
Pymble, NSW, Australia

Richard T. Watson
Department of MIS
University of Georgia
Athens, GA, USA

ISSN 2196-8705   ISSN 2196-8713   (electronic)
Progress in IS
ISBN 978-3-030-72784-0   ISBN 978-3-030-72785-7   (eBook)
https://doi.org/10.1007/978-3-030-72785-7

Foreword

Informatics, the science of processing data and information, including the study of the representation, managing and communication of information in both natural and engineered systems, is very important to the shipping and transport community. This is because it will ensure that our industry can obtain the full benefits of the current explosion in potential digital data sources and information technology developments that are the result of digitalisation.

BIMCO, as the world's largest direct-membership organisation for shipowners, charterers, shipbrokers and agents, understands the value of digitalisation of maritime informatics in supporting practical and flexible commercial agreements. Arrangements that are fair to all parties are vital to ensure sustainable and viable solutions. BIMCO currently has a strong focus on maritime digitalisation and is committed to making sure that appropriate standards and harmonisation are established to enable the huge potential of digital data to be realised.

Digitalisation is a catalyst for safety, security and environmental improvements, as well as an effective way to identify cost savings. For this reason, BIMCO, in association with the International Association of Ports and Harbors (IAPH), the International Cargo Handling Coordination Association (ICHCA), the International Chamber of Shipping (ICS), the International Harbour Masters' Association (IHMA), the International Maritime Pilots Association (IMPA), the International Port Community Systems Association (IPCSA), the International Ship Suppliers' Association (ISSA), the Federation of National Associations of Ship Brokers and Agents (FONASBA) and the PROTECT Group, has launched a call to action to accelerate digitalisation in the maritime domain and, by extension, further enable the power of maritime informatics.

As the Secretary-General and CEO of BIMCO, I am delighted to see this follow-on book on maritime informatics which contains more informative essays on current, practical examples of maritime informatics in action in support of sustainable maritime activities. The book is a very useful follow-up to the only recently published reference text *Maritime Informatics* and is edited by the same team of distinguished editors who have gathered more industry and academic experts to share their experience and insights on maritime digitalisation and maritime informatics.

BIMCO, Copenhagen, Denmark   David Loosley

Preface

Over the last decade, this book's editors have been involved in the shipping industry and in several European Union (EU) projects to improve the safety, efficiency and the sustainability of shipping. During this time, they realised that maritime informatics was an emergent specific thematic topic within information systems and raised it in their first book on the subject in late 2020. They see maritime informatics as:

- *The application of information systems to increase the efficiency, safety, resilience and ecological sustainability of the world's shipping industry*
- *An applied science, developed by data scientists to meet the needs of practice and applied by practitioners and data scientists cooperatively.*

Shipping is the world's oldest sharing economy and is conducted in a self-organising manner. Shipping is capital, energy and information intensive, and with the growing impact of digitalisation and climate change, there is a need to rethink the management and operations of this critical global industry—assisted by maritime informatics.

Building upon the inaugural book *Maritime Informatics* (Lind et al. 2021), this book focuses on several recent practical developments and experiences addressing broad industry concerns. It complements the first volume of *Maritime Informatics,* which provides a foundation for maritime informatics. In the first book, the authors identified the basic principles and the background activities and issues, as well as highlighting characteristics of the maritime sector that are specifically suited to digital transformation.

Noting that there is an ongoing need for a dedicated discourse on maritime informatics that unites researchers and practitioners in their efforts to improve the efficiency, safety, resilience and sustainability of shipping, this book continues that conversation.

Shipping, the most efficient way of transporting goods around the globe, handles about 90% of the world's trade. It enables regions and countries to exploit their comparative advantage and thus improves the lot of many citizens. Trade, facilitated by shipping and the application of Ricardo's comparative advantage principle, has created a global economy. The last few years, however, have demonstrated its fragility. Trade wars have flared up and the COVID-19 pandemic has demonstrated the brittleness of a highly interconnected society.

The sea has fascinated people for centuries. It has long been a source of transport, food and entertainment. However, with rising ocean temperatures, sea level increases and massive plastic waste in the ocean, we are endangering a major source of food and seaside cities will have to spend billions on adjusting to more frequent inundation. At the same time, aquaculture and windfarms are adding to our dependency on the seas. All these developments support the case for maritime informatics to help improve decision-making and analysis. We need to increase the quality of maritime decision-making to improve its efficiency, so that we achieve more with less, and in a sustainable way by minimising the environmental impact and improving safety, thereby protecting both human lives and the environment.

As we have learned, a digital society can be quite agile in some regards, such as the use of video conferencing and webinars for meetings in times of travel restrictions, but we still rely on people performing physical actions for many tasks, such as stocking supermarket shelves. It is likely that robots will take on many such physical operations to increase societal resilience, and there could be localisation of some operations that currently take advantage of labour arbitrage. The localisation possibilities of robots and such things as local 3D printing may then have an impact on shipping volumes. Identifying and reacting to these changes will be important. Maritime informatics will have an important role in identifying and predicting the changes and identifying the impacts.

Maritime informatics takes a holistic approach to shipping. Consequently, information requirements are strongly influenced by the self-organising nature of the shipping industry and the spatial-temporal data needed to manage a voyage and a port visit. Digital data streams are the fulcrum of coordination, because the many actors involved in a voyage and a port visit must share data in real time to organise the many associated activities. Influential voices in the shipping industry are promoting a digital transformation to raise the levels of transparency, predictability and visibility of all transport operations connected with shipping. There is a drive for enhanced situational awareness across the full spectrum of activities in the movement of goods from origin to destination.

The shipping industry has some particular cornerstones, which maritime informatics acknowledges, such as:

- Its self-organising nature, with perspectives and methods for perceiving multi-organisational activity (Watson et al. 2021)
- The concept of episodic tight coupling (Watson et al. 2021)
- The concept of a maritime stack (Watson et al. 2021)
- Balancing capital productivity (Watson 2020) and energy efficiency (Lind et al. 2020)
- The virtuous interplay between different types of systems (Haraldson et al. 2021; Watson 2020)

However, because of the high level of actor autonomy in this competitive industry, those who own and generate data want complete control over when they grant data access to others. Data owners tend only to authorise the sharing of data when it is in their self-interest, an issue discussed in this book. Much of the knowledge and practice for developing information systems is based upon building systems for internal use by an enterprise's employees. In this situation, data access authorisation is stable. For example, an employee's data access rights might persist for years, whereas, in shipping, authority to access particular data will likely be limited to a port visit or a portion of a visit. Thus, you have to set aside notions of building centralised databases and focus on digital data streams whose flow and attributes could be precisely managed.

The purpose of this book is to provide further background and insights into the current status and future directions of maritime informatics from the perspective of recent practical experiences, looking at such things as the supply chain in support of global emergencies, recycling resources and the circular economy, ports acting as multidimensional hubs, the standardisation of data, and the emergence of data sharing platforms in the global container trade.

Chapter 1: *Responding to humanitarian and global concerns with digitally enabled supply chain visibility* shows how data from the many involved actors and sources in the supply chain can provide (near) real-time situational awareness enabled by maritime informatics perspectives and methods. Supply chain operations can be complex, especially where multi-modal transport is at play, and where dynamic decision-making is required for the priority routing of goods in transit in the best interest of people and the planet. With digitally enabled supply chains, we can address many global concerns around today's environmental, social and economic challenges. Supply chain operations are pursued in an environment that can be characterised as a self-organising ecosystem. Connections between various (local) data sharing environments in networks of networks enable stakeholders in the supply chain to enhance their information base. Internet of things (IoT) technologies can complement the insights provided by data from various systems of records as to the whereabouts, status and conditions of goods and assets. Combining available data improves situational awareness, which enables efficient, green and humanitarian decision-making and facilitates a truly smooth and seamless movement of goods.

Chapter 2: *Digitalisation in a Maritime Circular Economy* introduces a framework for a digital foundation that could support a maritime circular economy exemplified by a circular material passport and a material pool. The increased strain on the Earth's resources may be mitigated by adopting the principles of the circular economy, particularly if these can be aligned with digital opportunities. The circular economy principles of redesigning the economic system to be restorative and regenerative are highly relevant to the maritime sector. A lot of the means used for sea transport and consequential port visits and cargo operations require physical infrastructures that both need to be utilised with high efficiency and should be reused as a whole or by its components in the secondary market. Reusing materials and securing high utilisation of physical infrastructures requires digital capabilities to underpin the circular economy business models, store the properties and track the use of physical infrastructures and other maritime assets. As the maritime industry increasingly captures the properties of material used for the ships, equipment and infrastructures necessary to fulfil sea transport as part of digitalisation, the sector seems to seize opportunities to make the move towards a digitally supported competitive maritime circularity that can both enhance and be guided by developments in maritime informatics.

Chapter 3: *Ports as multidimensional hubs* elaborates the role of the port as a manifold hub within the concept of maritime informatics. A port is described as a transport, information and energy hub, and the role of maritime informatics is exposed in this trifecta. The chapter also considers how ports of today can become the hubs of tomorrow, recognising both the existing mechanisms in place and maritime informatics as an enabler. Ports are complex ecosystems—multidimensional hubs that form a key piece in the puzzle of establishing and maintaining end-to-end transport chains. Effective port operations ensure that these chains are seamless, sustainable, resilient and predictable. Ports are a catalyst for synchronising the different transportation modes. They go beyond providing physical services to episodic visiting actors and other clients to encapsulating the capabilities of an integrated digital information hub. In addition, these multidimensional entities can support the storage and provision of "green" energy to enable a sustainable economic system. Maritime informatics is an enabler that helps ensure that physical services can be conducted as timely and efficiently as possible, so that a port's different stakeholders are able to coordinate their actions based on accurate predictions, and that the provision of resources to episodic tight coupled actors is done smoothly and without interruption.

Chapter 4: *The IMO reference data model: one solution fits most!* reviews technological advancements in the development and uptake potential of the International Maritime Organization (IMO) reference data model. In 2019, the IMO made it mandatory to support the electronic clearance of ships entering foreign ports. In preparation, the IMO Facilitation Committee started to develop a reference data model to harmonise the most important standards for ship clearance. The first version was published in 2020. The model is already extending into other areas of ship-port data exchanges, and it is now increasingly seen as a tool to coordinate development of new electronic data exchange standards for ship operations. The lack of such coordination has, up to now, been a significant problem—enhanced coordination is essential for the highly international shipping market.

Chapter 5: *The Role of Industry-based Standards Organisations in Digital Transformation* examines the various digitalisation and standardisation achievements of the Digital Container Shipping Association (DCSA), and compares them with similar activities by the International Air Transport Association (IATA), which has been instrumental in digitally transforming the airline industry—albeit over a longer period of time. The DCSA is a non-profit organisation that provides a collective voice for the largest shipping container lines. It seeks to complement intergovernmental organisations such as the UN Centre for Trade Facilitation and Electronic Business (UN/CEFACT) and the IMO, in particular by monitoring and contributing to practical data exchange standards necessary for business-to-business (B2B) interactions, as well as by providing a practitioners' perspective on the more general regulatory business to government (B2G) frameworks that the intergovernmental organisations are normally engaged in. The DCSA has established a number of key digital data transfer standards that have been adopted by the industry including track and trace, IoT, operational vessel schedules, just-in-time port call, electronic bill of lading (eBL)—as the first step towards eDocumentation—and cybersecurity.

Chapter 6: *Boosting the effectiveness of containerised supply chains: A case study of TradeLens* uses the implementation of a blockchain-based platform to identify the key data exchange issues currently being addressed in the containerised global transport trade, as well as identifying the overall potential and future challenges. These challenges include harmonising and making different data sharing platforms interoperable, the reluctance of some actors to share data and the potential for the role of customs agents and other actors to change as a result of digital data sharing.

<table>
<tr><td>Gothenburg, Sweden</td><td>Mikael Lind</td></tr>
<tr><td>Limassol, Cyprus</td><td>Michalis Michaelides</td></tr>
<tr><td>Pymble, NSW, Australia</td><td>Robert Ward</td></tr>
<tr><td>Athens, GA, USA</td><td>Richard T. Watson</td></tr>
</table>

References

Haraldson S, Lind M, Breitenbach S, Croston JC, Karlsson M, Hirtt G (2021) The port as a set of socio-technical systems: a multi-organisational view. In: Lind M, Michaelides MP, Ward R, Watson RT (eds) Maritime informatics. Springer, Heidelberg

Lind M, Michaelides MP, Ward R, Watson RT (eds) (2021) Maritime informatics. Springer, Heidelberg

Lind M, Watson R, Chua CP, Levy D, Theodossiou S, Primor O, Picco A (2020) A primer for a profitable and sustainable maritime business. Smart Maritime Network, 2020-09-09. https://smartmaritimenetwork.com/2020/09/09/prime-consid erations-for-shipping-success/

Watson RT (2020) Capital, systems and objects: the foundation and future of organizations. Springer, Heidelberg

Watson RT, Lind M, Delmeire N, Liesa F (2021) Shipping: a self-organising ecosystem. In: Lind M, Michaelides MP, Ward R, Watson RT (eds) Maritime informatics. Springer, Heidelberg

Contents

Editors and Contributors

About the Editors

Mikael Lind has been appointed by Chalmers University of Technology (M2) as the world's first professor in maritime informatics. He is also a Senior Strategic Research Advisor at Research Institutes of Sweden (RISE). He has initiated and headed a substantial part of several open innovation initiatives related to information and communication technologies for the sustainable transport of people and goods. He is substantially engaged in exploring the opportunity of maritime informatics as an applied research field. Lind serves as an expert for the World Economic Forum, Europe's Digital Transport Logistic Forum (DTLF) and UN/CEFACT. He has been the lead author of more than 60 concept notes associated with maritime informatics, and with over 10,000 LinkedIn connections and being well published in the maritime professional press, he has become a recognised thought leader in maritime informatics. He is based in Gothenburg, a major Scandinavian shipping centre that hosts a significant number of companies that offer information services to the maritime sector. Lind and Watson have been mini-track chairs for maritime informatics at the major regional IS conferences in Europe and the Americas for several years.

Michalis Michaelides is an Assistant Professor with the Department of Electrical Engineering, Computer Engineering and Informatics at the Cyprus University of Technology. Michalis' research interests include communication systems, wireless sensor networks, event detection and localisation, fault detection and diagnosis, fault tolerance, collaborative signal and information processing, computational intelligence with applications to environmental monitoring, intelligent systems and maritime informatics. Michalis has been involved as a principal investigator in many research projects, both local and European, including the Sea Traffic Management Validation (EU, 2016–2019) and STEAM (RPF, INTEGRATED/0916/0063, 2019–2021). In 2014, he received the Elsevier Building and Environment Journal Best Paper Award.

Robert Ward was the Secretary-General of the International Hydrographic Organization (IHO) until his retirement in 2017. Prior to that he was the Deputy Hydrographer of Australia. For more than 20 years, he represented Australia and subsequently the IHO at the highest international levels and has played an influential role in the development and implementation of global digital data exchange standards for nautical charting services that now also underpin the IMO's e-Navigation concept of a maritime digital information environment.

Richard T. Watson is a Regents Professor and the J. Rex Fuqua Distinguished Chair for Internet Strategy in the Terry College of Business at the University of Georgia. He is a former President of the Association for Information Systems (AIS). In 2011, he received the AIS's LEO award, which is given for exceptional lifetime achievement in information systems. He has written books on *Data Management; Electronic Commerce, Internet Strategy, Energy Informatics;* and *Capital, Systems, and Objects* and published nearly 200 journal articles, including articles in the major IS journals and practitioner journals such as *Harvard Business Review* and *California Management Review*. He was educated at the University of Western Australia (BSc, Dip. Comp), Monash University (MBA) and the University of Minnesota (PhD).

Contributors

J. Abril International Maritime Organization, London, UK

M. Munch Andersen University of Copenhagen, Frederiksberg, Denmark

G. Bapuji Women in Crisis Response LLC, Cambridge, MA, USA

H. Becha UN/CEFACT, Marseille, France

N. Bjørn-Andersen Copenhagen Business School, Frederiksberg, Denmark

J. Carson-Jackson The Nautical Institute, London, UK

N. D. Cauwer IPCSA, supported by Port of Antwerp, Antwerp, Belgium

F. Clary Agility, Washington, DC, USA

A. Dao e.circular ApS, Toronto, Canada

M. Fontanet International Maritime Organization, London, UK

J. Gardeichik Yaquina Consulting and Management, Rotterdam, The Netherlands

M. van Gogh World Economic Forum, Geneva, Switzerland

J. Th. Greven Netherlands Customs Administration, Apeldoorn, The Netherlands

S. Haraldson Research Institutes of Sweden (RISE), Gothenburg, Sweden

B. Hobson Circular and Sustainable Supply Chain Advisor, New York, NY, USA

H. Hvid Jensen e.circular ApS, Copenhagen, Denmark

J. S. Juhl BIMCO, Copenhagen, Denmark

N. Kouwenhouven IBM NL, Amsterdam, Netherlands

S. E. Larsen A.P. Moller – Maersk, Copenhagen, Denmark

W. Lehmacher Industrial Innovation Partners, Anchor Group, Geneva, Switzerland

M. Lind Research Institutes of Sweden (RISE), Chalmers University of Technology, Gothenburg, Sweden

J. Louw-Reimer Copenhagen Business School, Copenhagen, Denmark

E. Lund Sony Network Communications Europe, Lund, Sweden

R. Morton International Port Community Systems Association, London, UK

H. Mulder International Air Transport Association (IATA), Geneva, Switzerland

N. Murphy EVRYTHNG, Geneva, Switzerland

J. Liocouras Müller Nielsen Copenhagen Business School, Copenhagen, Denmark

V. Pandey DevopsInternational B.V., Amsterdam, The Netherlands

O. Pernia NextPort, Geneva, Switzerland

M. Petersen Kuehne Logistics University, Hamburg, Germany

S. Pettersson Research Institutes of Sweden (RISE), Chalmers University of Technology, Gothenburg, Sweden

S. Probert UN/CEFACT, Geneva, Switzerland

M. Renz Swedish Maritime Administration, Norrköping, Sweden

Ø. J. Rødseth SINTEF Ocean, Trondheim, Norway

H. Schleyerbach Digital Container Shipping Association (DCSA), Amsterdam, Netherlands

A. Simha MSC Mediterranean Shipping Company, Geneva, Switzerland

S. Singh The University of Trinidad and Tobago, Chaguaramas, Trinidad and Tobago

A. Turos 7 Chapters of Circularity, The Hague, The Netherlands

P. Zuesongdham Hamburg Port Authority, Hamburg, Germany

Abbreviations

3PL	Third-party logistics
API	Application programming interface
AN	Arrival notification
AI	Artificial intelligence
ASYCUDA	Automated System for Customs Data
B2B	Business to business
B2G	Business to government
BCO	Beneficial cargo owner
BPI	Bunkerspot Price Index
BRS	Business requirements specification
BSP-RDM	(UN/CEFACT) Buy-Ship-Pay Reference Data Model
Cargo IMP	(IATA) Cargo Interchange Message Procedures
CCL	(UN/CEFACT) Core Component Library
CEID	Circular economy identity and digital signature
CMPE	Circular Material Passport Engine
CSC	(IATA) Cargo Services Conference
ENS	(EU) Entry Summary Declarations
FAL	(IMO) Convention on Facilitation of International Maritime Traffic
DCPI	Data for Common Purpose Initiative
DCSA	Digital Container Shipping Association
DTLF	Digital Transport and Logistics Forum
DGMT	Digitizing Global Maritime Trade
e-AWB	e-Air Waybills
eBL	Electronic Bill of Lading
EDI	Electronic data interchange
EGDH	(IMO) Expert Group on Data Harmonization
EP	Exterior packaging
EPR	Extended producer responsibilities
FAL	(IMO) Facilitation Committee

GSBN	Global Shipping Business Network
GSSD	Global supply system dashboard
GHG	Greenhouse gas
HDX	Humanitarian Data Exchange
IRDM	IMO Reference Data Model
IEEE	Institute of Electrical and Electronics Engineers
IATA	International Air Transport Association
IALA	International Association of Aids to Navigation and Lighthouse Authorities
IAPH	International Association of Ports and Harbors
ICS	International Chamber of Shipping
IEC	International Electrotechnical Commission
IHO	International Hydrographic Organization
IMO	International Maritime Organization
ISO	International Organization for Standardization
IPCSA	International Port Community Systems Association
IoT	Internet of Things
JSON	JavaScript Object Notation
JIT	Just-in-time arrival
LNG	Liquefied natural gas
LSP	Logistics service providers
MDH	Maritime Declaration of Health
MEPC	(IMO) Maritime Environment Protection Committee
MSC	(IMO) Maritime Safety Committee
MSW	Maritime single window
MM	Materials Marketplace
NCSR	(IMO) Sub-committee on Navigation, Communication, Search and Rescue
NGO	Non-governmental organisation
OCHA	(UN) Office for the Coordination of Humanitarian Affairs
OPS	Onshore power system
OECD	Organisation for Economic Co-operation and Development
PortCDM	Port Collaborative Decision Making
PCS	Port community system
PMIS	Port Management Information Systems
PP	Proof provider
RPA	Robotics process automation
SCRDM	(UN/CEFACT) Supply Chain Reference Data Model
SDG	(United Nations) Sustainable Development Goal
SE	Sharing Economy
SMDG	Ship Message Design Group
TOS	Terminal operating system
UCC	(EU) Union Customs Code
UN/CEFACT	UN Centre for Trade Facilitation and Electronic Business

UN/EDIFACT	UN Electronic Data Interchange for Administration, Commerce and Transport
ICAO	(UN) International Civil Aviation Organization
UN	United Nations
UNLOCODE	United Nations Code for Trade and Transport Locations
UNECE	United Nations Economic Commission for Europe
VTS	Vessel traffic services
VDES	VHD Data Exchange System
WCO	World Customs Organization
WEF	World Economic Forum
WFP	World Food Programme
XML	Extensible Mark-up Language

Responding to Humanitarian and Global Concerns with Digitally Enabled Supply Chain Visibility

Wolfgang Lehmacher ⓘ, Mikael Lind ⓘ, Margi van Gogh ⓘ,
Hanane Becha ⓘ, Norbert Kouwenhoven ⓘ, Erik Lund ⓘ, Henk Mulder ⓘ,
André Simha ⓘ, Frank Clary, Mikael Renz ⓘ, and Niall Murphy ⓘ

W. Lehmacher (✉)
Industrial Innovation Partners, Anchor Group, Geneva/Zurich, Switzerland
e-mail: w.lehmacher@gmail.com

M. Lind
Research Institutes of Sweden (RISE), Chalmers University of Technology, Gothenburg,
Sweden
e-mail: mikael@realsearchers.com

M. van Gogh
Supply Chain and Transport Industries, World Economic Forum, Geneva, Switzerland
e-mail: Margi.VanGogh@weforum.org

H. Becha
UN/CEFACT Transport and Logistics, Marseille, France
e-mail: hbecha@gmail.com

N. Kouwenhoven
IBM NL, Amsterdam, The Netherlands
e-mail: Norbert.kouwenhoven@nl.ibm.com

E. Lund
Sony Network Communications Europe, Lund, Sweden
e-mail: erik.lund@sony.com

H. Mulder
International Air Transport Association (IATA), Geneva, Switzerland
e-mail: mulderh@iata.org

A. Simha
MSC Mediterranean Shipping Company, Geneva, Switzerland
e-mail: andre.simha@msc.com

F. Clary
Agility, Washington, DC, USA
e-mail: fclary@agility.com

M. Renz
Swedish Maritime Administration, Norrköping, Sweden
e-mail: mikael.renz@sjofartsverket.se

M. Lind et al. (eds.), *Maritime Informatics*, Progress in IS,
https://doi.org/10.1007/978-3-030-72785-7_1

1 Introduction: Maritime Informatics for Global Situational Awareness

Every instance of a transport process is unique in time and most often the routes a shipment takes are also unique, end-to-end. While it might be that the pattern of intermodal transport appears the same for repeating journeys, even then, the various transport units involved rely on different and usually variable resources and conditions under the control of individual entities, making every journey unique. It might be a particular transport operator needing to vary a certain means of transport or use a different transhipment hub, for example. Transport operations to ensure supply in areas of disaster or conflict are by definition purpose-built.

The different systems supporting an engaged actor, or communities of actors interacting with each other, need to be connected to each other to facilitate tight episodic coupling (Watson et al. 2021) by the actors being engaged in local and horizontal information sharing communities (Lind et al. 2020d).

Maritime Informatics provides the opportunity to manage the necessary collaborative alignment (Lind et al. 2020a) to create and monitor those transport chains in an efficient and visible manner. However, as the maritime transport sector is highly self-organising and interdependent it is also important to seek applications where plans and information about progress, and disruptions, are aggregated beyond a single actor and their local ecosystems. Such aggregations of coarse-grained real-time situational awareness enable transport coordinators, Logistics Service Providers (LSP), carriers and Beneficial Cargo Owners (BCO) to follow the transport flow and to intervene when the transport plan is not meeting intentions.

2 Everybody Wants to Know More

Data and information are the foundation of insight. Substantial investments today are being made in digital technologies allowing for more digital data streams in supply chains. LSPs, carriers, intermodal operators (air, sea, ground, etc.), port authorities and terminal operators, regulatory bodies, BCOs and data providers as well as software companies are all working on this topic. The European Commission forecasts exponential growth of data streams (EC 2020) and is setting up legislation aiming at improving data flows between actors (EC Data strategy).

Efficient routing and high utilisation of logistics assets and infrastructure lead to commercial and environmental efficiency benefits. This includes the efficient use of vessels, planes, trucks, barges and trains, as well as loading/unloading equipment. Episodically visiting actors are served just-in-time with short turn-around times at transhipment hubs, reducing waiting times and costs to a minimum. All of these

N. Murphy
EVRYTHNG, Geneva, Switzerland
e-mail: niall@evrythng.com

require the sharing of information about the conditions and movements of goods as the basis for visibility and transparency.

Visibility and transparency are critical for condition and time sensitive goods, like vaccines, fresh foods and flowers, and for bringing efficiency, agility, resilience, and predictability into the supply chain. Such visibility and transparency require a range of data, including cargo requirements, the location of shipments and assets, the temperature and shock conditions goods are exposed to, and also the situations merchandise face along the supply chain, like port congestion or bad weather.

As a result of Covid-19 restrictions across the globe, the number of people facing starvation due to food insecurity at the beginning of 2020 has doubled from a projected 135 million to more than 270 million by the end of the year. According to a July 2020 Oxfam Report, this could result in 6000–12,000 deaths per day.

Transparency is a must to improve emergency and humanitarian support, such as with the Covid-19 pandemic. Flagging a container 'humanitarian prio' in a truly transparent supply chain would make it visible for all relevant supply chain participants thereby allowing priority treatment to speed up movement and delivery, and pre-emptively circumvent disruptions in the system. With the right infrastructure in place, a carrier could put such a container on deck, the terminal could off-load it first, customs could fast-track clearance or clear the container while still at sea, the port could even make sure all the traffic lights in the port are set to green for the haulier's truck, etc. This kind of data process and physical flow integration is already in use in the retail, electronic, food and fashion industries wherein some orders are prioritised and accelerated through the chain.

In particular, the distribution of a Covid-19 vaccine is a logistics challenge that has never been faced before. The optimisation of the limited and constrained air cargo capacity (due to the Covid-19 pandemic grounding many passenger aircraft that also carry cargo) and the disrupted ocean freight market (due to port congestion and container imbalances) as well as the limited cold chain infrastructure, combined with the relatively short expiration dates of vaccines means that increased visibility and transparency of vaccine supply chain data, from shipper, to transport providers, hospital, doctors and citizens literally equates to more lives saved.

More visibility and transparency aid 'green decision making' on mode choices and routings. Optimised routes and flows produce less carbon emissions. Supply chain visibility is an important ingredient for true global and human benefits to be realised (Lind et al. 2020e). Visibility also allows for post transport analyses and the verification of freight charges. Price-gouging or excesses in supply chains would be more easily exposed.

Ports and hinterland carriers want to know what cargo is approaching, when it will arrive, and where it is heading after unloading. Governments need to know what materials are moving, where, when, and how, and their origin. Customs authorities need to know what goods are imported and exported. All share the need for data, and all want to know more.

3 The Way Forward: Connecting Actors in a Network of Networks Setting

Situational awareness can be derived from combining the data that each involved BCO, LSP, carrier or government agency shares. There are many sources for these data, such as IoT devices, smart containers, and systems of records for engaging LSPs that provide data on agreements, location and conditions within a system of production. There are many means to share, varying from central databases, such as the UNCTAD Automated System for Customs Data (ASYCUDA) "Digitizing Global Maritime Trade" (DGMT) project (UNCTAD 2020), ASYCUDA Single Windows, shared blockchain ledgers, and there are various methods to control this sharing to determine who can see what and when.

Initiatives such as the International Air Transport Association (IATA) ONE Record, building upon the Internet of Logistics, or the TradeLens data sharing environment, originating from collaboration between Maersk and IBM, are two efforts to create a network of (local) networks. Within the European initiative of the Digital Transport Logistic Forum (DTLF),[1] concepts for a federated environment of networks of networks are now emerging and being validated within the FEDeRATED and FENIX projects. There are also integrated customs clearance solutions being used in many emerging markets such as Kenya, Pakistan, Ghana, Tanzania, and others.

Multiple entities within the consumer, supply chain and logistics arena are exploring the concept of data aggregation for the common good. Essentially, bringing the least granular level of anonymised data from multiple open and closed network sources (and existing aggregator platforms) together in a non-commercial, open-source global supply system dashboard (GSSD), providing system-wide visibility on the movement of essential goods to vulnerable communities served by the humanitarian sector. Further, we now see the introduction of such things as smart containers (IoT), (Becha et al. 2020) as a source of data that cuts across the different modes of transport. We are also seeing the power of artificial intelligence being used by ocean carriers to review submitted information and documents to look for safety, security, and trade compliance deficiencies. Innovation and new opportunities are arising; for all stakeholders along the supply chain, including trade financiers, risk managers, and insurance companies, but also for software vendors and data and intelligence providers.

[1]www.dtlf.eu.

4 Benefits Within Reach

When parties decide to collaborate and agree to mutually share data about a shipment, the benefits are huge: Increased visibility and transparency, integrated performance (because actions pursued by all actors are continually coordinated and synchronised throughout the supply chain) administrative preparedness of latter parts of the transport chain before actual physical operations occur, reduced waiting time, secured fulfilment levels, minimised administrative burden, collaboration regardless of location, data point accuracy, cost effectiveness, increased resilience, higher levels of safety and less accidents and casualties, less carbon and other emissions, more innovation, improved and new services, capabilities for predictive and collective actions, enabled post transport analytics, real time decision making, and increased automation.

Imagine a situation where the many actors, operating across and among the different modes of transport, provided minimum levels of data to enable decisions on the prioritisation of transport, collaboratively reducing delays and waste, increasing the number of lives protected. Envision analyses of areas of extreme poverty and famine; food, medicines and medical equipment arriving faster to save lives.

The value of these benefits for the stakeholder along the supply chain, society and the planet offsets the effort required for the upgrades of the current systems and practices.

5 Challenges to Overcome

The transport ecosystem is reliant on many autonomous actors. Sometimes they are competitors chasing the same customers, yet at other times the same players seek to collaborate to reap the benefits of co-opetition. This co-opetition is usually sub-optimal. To overcome this, local data sharing communities have emerged to improve performance. Port Community Systems, Government Single Windows, Trader Community platforms are examples of this sort of development. One issue here is to allow for the co-existence of multiple platforms, both as local and horizontal data sharing communities (Lind et al. 2020b).

Several specific requirements and challenges need to be taken into account to improve data sharing across communities and networks of (local) networks, including:

- Overcoming resistance to new business models
- A need to lower the thresholds for any actor to become digitally included
- Establishing agreed way(s) for identifying the cargo being transported, with different levels of granularity
- Addressing the automatic fear of data sharing, even when it will be protected by robust data sharing rules and governance models
- Overcoming the misconception that withholding non-sensitive data will create a sustainable competitive advantage

- Substantiating data sharing trust and security models between role players
- Lack of interoperability and standardised messaging and interfacing between information sharing communities
- Many different formats and standards on data transmission.

6 Moving Ahead

The challenges can be overcome through building communities and by developing technologies that will provide immediate financial benefit to supply chain stakeholders. This will ensure fast adoption and create the basis for enabling situational awareness along the chain. Data aggregation in many shapes and forms will contribute to the effort. Standards will help to exchange data in an efficient way. The combination of all these factors will help economic growth but they also assist and enhance global and humanitarian efforts. Fighting climate change and ensuring supply in a disaster situation will also benefit from more transparency and the ability to better collaborate across supply chain ecosystems.

Data governance frameworks can help to overcome concerns and intuitive reluctance to sharing data. The Data for Common Purpose Initiative (DCPI) at the World Economic Forum (2020) focuses on creating a new flexible data governance model. The view is that data can and should be treated differently depending on its actual and anticipated use, and that today's *Fourth Industrial Revolution* smart technologies can enable differentiated 'permission-ing' of the same data, dependent upon context.

6.1 Connected Information Sharing Communities Enabling Information Transparency

In a transport and logistics chain, data sharing is most often conducted in multiple local communities. These could be geographically delimited, such as in implementations of the Port Collaborative Decision Making (PortCDM) concept, port community systems, national Single Window implementation, or a configuration of a set of actors sharing a common concern. An example of the latter is the collaboration among shipping lines to exchange schedules and progress in movements thereby allowing for exchanging time slots for port visits, canal transits and similar access. Another example is the open collaboration needed for eBill of Lading which has become a key differentiator during the Covid-19 crisis (Lind et al. 2020d).

The increasing volume of maritime data and number of platforms help to improve the coordination and synchronisation along the maritime value chain, as well as associated transport chains. An increasing number of supply chain stakeholders, and especially in relation to port operations, is resulting in a redefinition of the role that different actors, such as the ship agent, (Lind and Croston 2020) take in assuring sustainable maritime transport operations. This trend also provides possibilities and incentives for ports to establish themselves as transhipment hubs and thereby improve their interactions with shipping lines and hinterland operators.

Several initiatives are underway to establish communities empowered by data sharing platforms (data pipelines) (Lind et al. 2020d). One initiative is to adopt message standards and standardised interfaces for the exchange of relevant information of mutual interest and benefit; another option is the provision of operational data sharing environments (Becha et al. 2020).

Today, diverse communities are surfacing in different forms joining different stakeholders engaged in a delimited setting. One can think of these implementations as data sharing communities utilising one-to-many communication. In the following figure, the combination of local (a port), horizontal (across a supply chain), and regulatory (Maritime Single Window) data sharing communities are depicted (Lind et al. 2020d; Lind and Renz 2020). These different types of inter-related communities each constitute an important feed for horizontal information sharing by connecting communities (Fig. 1), such as TradeLens (Louw-Reimer et al. 2021).

Most data sharing platforms come with directories or catalogues akin to "yellow pages" that are used to expose the diverse services provided to the community. These encourage new participants to join the community.

6.2 Enabling Situational Awareness Along the Supply Chain

For BCOs, LSPs and carriers to make accurate plans and manage disruptions, it is essential for them to have insights and situational awareness of what is planned and happening along the supply chain that is not within the scope of actions they control. Situational awareness can be defined simply as "knowing what is going on around us", or—more technically—as "the perception of the elements in the environment within a volume of time and space, the comprehension of their meaning and the projection of their status in the near future" (Endsley 1995).

Situational awareness is essential for tackling humanitarian and global concerns. These concerns go beyond the value production made by a single actor. Each of the stakeholders has some pieces of the puzzle, but to ensure a holistic view of the status of the transport chain, the different entities need to report what they know.

In order to achieve this however, there are some essential pieces that need to be put in place, such as:

- Message standards for the information that participating actors find incentives to share
- Standardised interfaces, APIs, allowing for digital data exchanges to be conducted
- Identifiable nodes in the network, such as the IATA One Record model, operating in a standardised way and constituting a web of digital transport nodes.

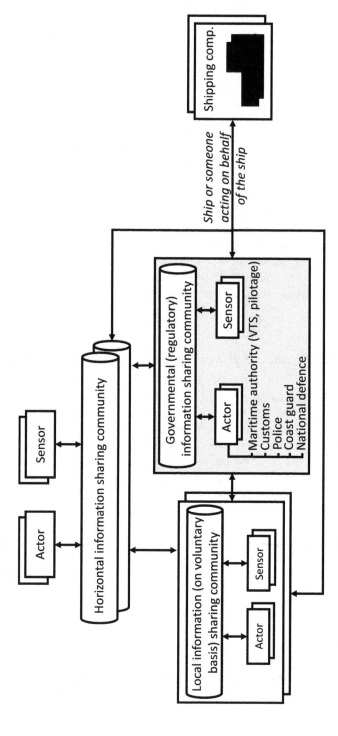

Fig. 1 Connected information sharing communities (Lind et al. 2020d; Lind and Renz 2020)

The situational awareness emerging from data sharing along the supply chain constitutes components of the situational awareness needed by all stakeholders.

6.3   Data Aggregation for the Common Good

The insights drawn from combined data can serve the common good. Full transparency of the contents of the world's containers (sea and air) could provide deep insights into various dimensions. The whereabouts of vaccines, for example, can help to identify logistic bottlenecks and remove them rapidly.

Another example is where analysing the world's cargo flows can reveal areas of poverty, or zones without access to specific food or medicines. Insight can help to identify and improve faulty supply chains to combat wastage, address poverty and enable new opportunities for wealth creation, as has been seen in several cases across the African continent, where understanding and improving the logistical needs and capabilities has reduced food wastage from farm to market and created new export, income and wealth creation opportunities.

Increased transparency also has a downside: it can be misused. In unleashing the potential of having access to aggregated data, data sovereignty is extremely important. What seems a common good to one, can be seen as 'big brother watching' by another. Access to all citizens' health files can be a blessing for virus fighting, but can be misused by employers who seek to avoid hiring people with, for example, an HIV history. Access to all citizens' income statements can be a blessing for a tax agency or anti-money laundering organisations, but can be misused by criminals to find wealthy targets.

Data aggregators should meticulously keep track of the source and ownership of the data that they receive. For every data element or set of data used, the owner has to approve the access. Only then can the interests of individuals and companies be protected and the risk of the punitive use of data against supply chain actors be mitigated. Achieving this goal requires an extensive set of measures and a collaborative approach worldwide.

First and foremost, the right to own your data has to be acknowledged and protected by law. Secondly, every service provider has to arrange for proper approval to use data. Protecting data requires strict access rules at an aggregator level, and these rules have to be enforced. Technical measures such as strict login procedures, access protocols, and data encryption need to be ensured. Permanent monitoring and fraud fighting have to be executed by the aggregators. Third, governments need to implement appropriate legislation and an accompanying enforcement strategy. Audits and inspections are indispensable prerequisites. Finally, special arrangements have to be made for aggregators and service providers that operate across borders.

6.4   The Necessity of Standards

Standards (national, regional or global) are the fruit of collective efforts to guarantee interoperability. Standards organisations, through which participants from different segments of the industry collaborate, are among the few places where competitors work side-by-side in a safe place to do so from an anti-trust perspective. The standardization process ensures that all voices are heard, standardisation efforts do not favour particular commercial interests, and the resulting standards have the consensus-derived support of the diverse and representative participants. Standards development contributors usually comprise industry experts, technology companies and customers representing all fields of the economy.

Getting the inside view enables businesses to anticipate major waves of innovation and ensure that their business strategies remain in tune with this innovation. The European Commission has identified the use of standards as a mechanism of innovation sharing, European competitiveness and further economic integration within the Union (The European Digital Strategy). Standards create efficiencies and economies of scale that ultimately result in lower costs to all stakeholders. Companies developing standards-based products and services can gain access to global markets. Standards can be revised to meet industry needs and remain relevant over time. They can enable next-generation technologies by supporting backward compatibility and protecting past investments while creating the confidence to continue investing in the digital solutions.

The maritime industry relies on technical standards to an extent rivalled by few other industries. Containerisation shifted shipping from a labour and handling intensive process into an efficient and partially automated industry that slashed the cost of transporting goods around the world and drove the boom in global trade. Tireless efforts of standardisation made it possible for almost any container to travel across the various modes of transport on road vehicles, trains, and ships.

With the ramp-up of new and emerging technologies, standards are more necessary than ever. With the use of IoT technologies in the maritime logistic value chain, namely smart containers, the need to create further standards has arisen. Nowadays, the carriers and the terminal operators have to play the role of network providers on the top of their traditional functions (Becha 2019).

The United Nations Centre for Trade Facilitation and Electronic Business (UN/CEFACT) standardisation effort (Becha 2020) is one of many emerging initiatives (Lind et al. 2020c) supporting global trade. Standards-based data exchange usage increases the ability to collaborate, which in turn increases efficiency. Additionally, such standards reduce development and deployment costs and cut time to market for Internet of Things (IoT) solution providers. Data exchange standards developed in an open process arena offer a useful aid to all parties interested in the technical applications and implementation of smart solutions.

Standards reduce the risk of developing proprietary technologies with significant deployment limitations and the lack of interoperability among systems and devices.

Furthermore, standards enable the parties to avoid costly and time-consuming integration and limit the risk of vendor lock-in.

As an example, the UN/CEFACT Smart Container Business Requirements Specification (BRS) ensures that the various ecosystem actors share a common understanding of smart container benefits by presenting various use cases. It also details the smart container data elements (UN/CEFACT 2019). Defining the data elements that smart containers can generate accelerates integration and the use of smart container data on different platforms for the enhancement of operations. The focus of the UN/CEFACT Smart Container project is to define the data elements via varied use cases. Smart containers will revolutionise the capture and timely reporting of data throughout the supply chains. They are an essential building block to meet the emerging requirements for end-to-end supply chain visibility (Lind et al. 2021) and to deliver the needed Application Programming Interfaces (APIs) for a simpler integration of data in third party solutions.

There is also a need to harmonise standards that are overlapping, and to simplify the data flowing among participants and across different modes of transport. Standards can overlap at any logistic hub and on any level. One such large initiative is the reference data model (Cauwer et al. 2021) adopted by the International Maritime Organization (IMO) also involving the World Customs Organization (WCO), UN/CEFACT and ISO created in order to harmonise and translate between the standards developed by these organization. The work is published in the IMO Compendium on Facilitation and Electronic Business and has been ratified by approximately 130 countries.

7 Coming Together to Respond to Humanitarian and Planetary Concerns

Maritime informatics can help in many ways to reduce the burden on people and the planet. Mainly through establishing visibility, supporting coordination, and improving planning and supply chain decision making.

7.1 Tackling Global Concerns

The ability to monitor the flows along safe and environmentally-friendly circular supply chains that support the circular economy concept could help reduce CO_2 emissions, enable the reuse of certain components, and fight illegal waste dumping. Better planning and more efficient supply chain networks will serve the common good by reducing pollution and the waste of energy and other resources.

One major global concern is the greenhouse gas (GHG) emissions of the maritime industry. The IMO GHG strategy has set the goal to reduce the sector's annual greenhouse gas emissions by 50% of 2008 levels by 2050, aligning with the Paris Agreement on climate change.

Several initiatives support the realisation of this objective. One effort is the Getting to Zero Coalition,[2] an alliance of more than 120 companies within the maritime, energy, infrastructure and finance sectors, supported by key governments and prominent non-governmental international organisations. The Coalition aims at operating commercially viable zero-emission vessels powered by zero-emission fuels by 2030. This partnership between the Global Maritime Forum, the Friends of Ocean Action, and the World Economic Forum, include the Port of Antwerp in Belgium, Port of Aarhus in Denmark, Port of Rotterdam in the Netherlands and Vancouver Fraser Port Authority in Canada. The Getting to Zero Coalition builds among others upon the Poseidon Principles, a global framework for climate-aligned ship financing, which was also launched in 2019. Capturing the full potential of these efforts requires to include data sharing in the concept. The respective capabilities are in the process of being built.

Different regulators are tracking vessel-level fuel consumption and emissions, as well as vessel efficiency. Organisations provide data to improve supply chain performance as well as environmental impact. Integrating consumption and emissions data is required to achieve improved cost/carbon efficiency (Lind et al. 2020f). There are a number of data aggregators and utilities that are providing trade-lane level emissions forecasts for planning, as well as CO_2 estimates for shipper or BCO, LSP and carrier reporting. Researchers[3] and technology developers[4] are using satellite and sensor data to monitor vessel emissions as observed from satellites, also to identify and take measures against overfishing and illegal fishing (Park et al. 2021).

7.2   The Humanitarian Response

Operating platforms help collaboration and dynamic coordination along the supply chain during crisis situations. Asset tracking and shipment monitoring tools provide data that allow for dynamic decision making and action in the case of supply chain divergence, excursions and other disruptions. Data on situational awareness allows for the different actors involved to collaboratively align (Lind et al. 2020a).

As conditions may be highly challenging, caused by extreme weather, infrastructure damage, lack of capacity and human labour, every bit of data counts in a crisis situation. Therefore, it is important to digitise preparedness information so that it is available to all that need it, when they need it. Such preparedness means a never-ending chase for identifying scenarios that cover "how shall we act if this

---

[2]https://www.globalmaritimeforum.org/getting-to-zero-coalition/.

[3]https://phys.org/news/2019-11-satellite-tracking-ships-affect-clouds.html.

[4]https://www.ghgsat.com/.

happens?" informed by what has historically happened and the possible means being at hand.

The United Nations Global Logistics Cluster and United Nations World Food Programme (WFP) have developed a number of data sources and modelling tools that can assist humanitarian actors in preparing for emergencies—as well as responding to them. The Cluster's Preparedness Platform[5] is an example of the power of data in humanitarian emergencies. "Developed as a dynamic and innovative digital data collection tool, the platform (currently in test phase) combines imagery, mapping, analytics and real-time reporting to improve decision making for preparedness and response." The tool is envisioned to combine risk and response information, such as road network functionality, available capacities, and local needs.

Another example of the importance of information is the Logistics Capacity Assessment,[6] wherein humanitarian and private sector actors provide local capacities and constraints information for critical supply chain elements such as ports, airports, roads, railroads, fuel, telecommunication, and other infrastructure and resources.

A third humanitarian data source under development is the Humanitarian Data Exchange (HDX) platform,[7] wherein the United Nations Office for the Coordination of Humanitarian Affairs (OCHA) aggregates data from a wide range of sources. The HDX platform has the capability of integrating any type of data set and making it available to humanitarian action stakeholders, including public and private sector actors.

Digital marketplaces can facilitate the matching of supply and demand. Crypto currencies enable the acceleration of support and the tracing of financial aid. The emerging digitalised humanitarian supply ecosystem also enables post event analysis.

Finally, in humanitarian action an important consideration is data privacy. HDX has been utilising data since 2018 to inform decision-making at various occasions. These include human displacement in South Sudan, and the Ebola outbreak in the Democratic Republic of Congo. While access to data is crucial to ensure smooth operation in a crisis situation, the poor information management may spark violence and discrimination in situations of persecution. Groups and individuals risk being targets, even when they are not directly identifiable, such as following the publication of a report or a situation analysis. Failure to ensure data confidentiality may lead to stigma and threaten the actors' reputations, putting both employees and beneficiaries at risk. Therefore, it is essential that the stakeholders involved in humanitarian action, such as international organisations (IOs), non-governmental organisations (NGOs), charities and volunteer groups, as well as businesses and governments, respect the fundamental principles of data protection and adopt relevant policies, procedures and precautions when providing humanitarian assistance

---

[5]https://logcluster.org/preparedness.

[6]https://logcluster.org/lcas.

[7]humdata.org.

around the globe (Gazi 2020). In 2016, the United Nations Office for the Coordination of Humanitarian Affairs (UN OCHA) published an initial data privacy standards and guidance document, which is continually being updated.[8]

It is important to point out that so far, a system-wide, open-source visibility platform to aid humanitarian efforts is still missing. Aggregating elements of private and public data from commodity, transport and disruption monitoring sources is required to improve system-wide resilience, enabling agile responses to improve outcomes for communities suffering in the face of humanitarian crises.

We are in need of frameworks that effectively protect the individual, while allowing the individual and the community to harness the full value of data. The Data for Common Purpose Initiative (DCPI) of the World Economic Forum aims at a flexible data governance model that allows for the combining of data from personal, commercial, and government sources, while still protecting rights. This will also positively empower a variety of stakeholders and remove unintended policy barriers. The DCPI is built on the belief that orienting data policy and data models around common purposes, such as specific use cases, will unlock opportunities for both the public good and commercial spheres. DCPI utilises use cases to demonstrate key hypotheses. The Colombia Moonshot (facilitating a government-led data marketplace) is one such pilot. Facilitating data marketplaces will promote the exchange of data as a strategic asset for common good and stimulate the transition from a traditional to a data-driven economy (WEF 2020).

Increasing data sharing initiatives suggest that aspirations for a platform enabling global supply system visibility is well within reach. Collaborations that result in elements of data being shared and used for common good presents both a noble and necessary use case.

8   Summary and Call for Action

Quantifiable economic, environmental, and societal benefits originate from sharing data. However, the foundations are yet to be fully established and there are challenges to overcome.

As a result of increasing digital data sharing activity, the maritime sector is now establishing a new discipline of maritime informatics[9] (Lind et al. 2020c) that unites practitioners and academics to jointly contribute to making shipping more efficient, sustainable and resilient, empowered by digital data sharing. At the core is to ensure a balance between capital productivity and energy efficiency (Lind et al. 2020f) enabling dynamic decision making for optimised resource utilisation based on enhanced predictability. Due to similarities between the multi-modal transport chain and maritime supply chains, maritime informatics provides a promising

---

[8]https://data.humdata.org/dataset/2048a947-5714-4220-905b-e662cbcd14c8/resource/c7053042-fd68-44c7-ae24-a57890a48235/download/ocha-dr-guidelines-working-draft-032019.pdf.
[9]www.maritimeinformatics.org.

discourse to develop and implement the necessary instruments needed for enabling a change.

Foundational is the need to motivate an attitudinal shift: In the interest of humanity and the planet, everyone should take responsibility for promoting data sharing, and all need to help establish simple and fair data sharing protocols. For every player there needs to be a benefit—a commercial or social reward. Only then will the true potential of data sharing be achieved.

It is not a question of which platform should be used. It is not a question of withholding data waiting for monetisation or a competitive edge. Our call for action is for a collaborative effort to share data, under mutually agreed and fair sharing conditions. This is urgent for the future of our society, vulnerable communities, the maritime industry and also our planet!

References

Becha H (2019) Standardization supporting global trade, edn. 91. Port Technology International. https://www.porttechnology.org/editions/shipping-2020-a-vision-for-tomorrow/

Becha H (2020) The UN/CEFACT Smart Container project. The magazine of international Institute of Marine Surveying, issue 91, March 2020. https://www.iims.org.uk/wpcontent/uploads/2020/02/The-Report-March-2020.pdf

Becha H, Frazier T, Lind M, Schröder M, Voorspuij J (2020) Smart containers and situational awareness. Smart Maritime Network, 12 Aug 2020. https://smartmaritimenetwork.com/2020/08/12/the-cargo-owners-case-for-smart-containers/

Cauwer ND, Fontanet M, Abril J, Greven JT, Juhl JS, Probert S, Renz M, Rødseth ØJ (2021) The IMO reference data model—one solution fits most! In: Lind M, Michaelides M, Ward R, Watson RT (eds) Maritime informatics: additional perspectives and applications. Springer, Heidelberg

EC (2020) A European strategy for data. Communication from the Commission to the European Parliament, The Council, The European Economic and Social Committee and the Committee of the Regions. https://ec.europa.eu/info/sites/info/files/communication-european-strategy-data-19feb2020_en.pdf

Endsley MR (1995) Toward a theory of situation awareness in dynamic systems. Hum Factors 37 (1):32–64

Gazi T (2020) Data to the rescue: how humanitarian aid NGOs should collect information based on the GDPR. J Int Humanit Action. https://doi.org/10.1186/s41018-020-00078-0

Lind M, Croston JC (2020) Rethinking maritime businesses for the digital age: the evolving role of ship agents. Article No. 49 [UNCTAD Transport and Trade Facilitation Newsletter N°85—First Quarter 2020]. https://unctad.org/en/pages/newsdetails.aspx?OriginalVersionID=2306

Lind M, Renz M (2020) Do maritime authorities have a role in digitalization of shipping?—the "Digital (port)Approach" in a sea transport context. https://smartmaritimenetwork.com/wp-content/uploads/2020/07/The-digital-approach-in-context.pdf

Lind M, Becha H, Simha A, Bottin F, Larsen SE (2020a) Smart decision-making and collaborative alignment. Smart Maritime Network, 20 Aug 2020. https://smartmaritimenetwork.com/2020/08/20/smart-decision-making-and-collaborative-alignment/

Lind M, Becha H, Simha A, Bottin F, Larsen SE (2020b) Digital containerisation. Smart Maritime Network, 18 June 2020. https://smartmaritimenetwork.com/wp-content/uploads/2020/06/Information-transparency-through-standardised-messaging-and-interfacing.pdf

Lind M, Watson R, Hoffmann J, Ward R, Michaelides M (2020c) Maritime Informatics: an emerging discipline for a digitally connected efficient, sustainable and resilient industry. Article No. 59 [UNCTAD Transport and Trade Facilitation Newsletter N°87—Third Quarter 2020]. https://unctad.org/en/pages/newsdetails.aspx?OriginalVersionID=2456

Lind M, Simha S, Becha H (2020d) Creating value for the transport buyer with Digital Data Streams. The Maritime Executive, 9 Mar 2020. https://maritime-executive.com/editorials/creating-value-for-the-transport-buyer-with-digital-data-streams

Lind M, van Gogh M, Becha H, Kouwenhoven N, Lehmacher W, Lund E, Mulder H, Murphy N, Simha A (2020e) Information sharing communities for digitally enabled supply chain visibility. Article No. 64 [UNCTAD Transport and Trade Facilitation Newsletter N°88—Fourth Quarter 2020]. https://unctad.org/news/information-sharing-communities-digitally-enabled-supply-chain-visibility

Lind M, Watson R, Chua CP, Levy D, Theodossiou S, Primor O, Picco A (2020f) A primer for a profitable and sustainable maritime business. Smart Maritime Network, 9 Sept 2020. https://smartmaritimenetwork.com/2020/09/09/prime-considerations-for-shipping-success/

Lind M, Ward R, Hvid JH, Chua CP, Simha A, Karlsson J, Göthberg L, Penttinen T, Theodosiou DP (2021) The future of shipping—collaboration through digital data sharing. In: Lind M, Michaelides M, Ward R, Watson RT (eds) Maritime informatics. Springer, Heidelberg

Louw-Reimer J, Nielsen JLM, Bjørn-Andersen N, Kouwenhoven N (2021) TradeLens—a case study on boosting the effectiveness of containerised supply chains. In: Lind M, Michaelides M, Ward R, Watson RT (eds) Maritime informatics: additional perspectives and applications. Springer, Heidelberg

Park JH, Lind M, Bjørn-Andersen N, Christensen T, von Elern F, Pot FW (2021) Maritime Informatics for recreational and fishing vessels. In: Lind M, Michaelides M, Ward R, Watson RT (eds) Maritime informatics. Springer, Heidelberg

UN/CEFACT (2019) The UN/CEFACT Smart Container Business Specifications (BRS). https://www.unece.org/fileadmin/DAM/cefact/brs/BRS-SmartContainer_v1.0.pdf

UNCTAD (2020) 'Digitizing Global Maritime Trade' project launched. https://unctad.org/news/digitizing-global-maritime-trade-project-launched

Watson RT, Lind M, Delmeire N, Liesa F (2021) Shipping: a self-organising ecosystem. In: Lind M, Michaelides M, Ward R, Watson RT (eds) Maritime informatics. Springer, Heidelberg

WEF (2020) Data for Common Purpose Initiative (DCPI), World Economic Forum. https://www.weforum.org/projects/data-for-common-purpose-initiative-dcpi

Digitalisation in a Maritime Circular Economy

Henrik Hvid Jensen ⓘ, Maj Munch Andersen ⓘ, Anh Dao ⓘ, Mikael Lind ⓘ, Vikas Pandey ⓘ, Godha Bapuji ⓘ, Moritz Petersen ⓘ, Bettina Hobson ⓘ, Wolfgang Lehmacher ⓘ, and Attila Turos ⓘ

H. H. Jensen (✉)
e.circular ApS, Copenhagen, Denmark
e-mail: henrikhvidjensen@gmail.com

M. M. Andersen
University of Copenhagen, Frederiksberg, Denmark
e-mail: Mma@ign.ku.dk

A. Dao
e.circular ApS, Toronto, Canada
e-mail: ann.dao.bayer@gmail.com

M. Lind
Research Institutes of Sweden (RISE) and Chalmers University of Technology, Gothenburg, Sweden
e-mail: mikael@realsearchers.com

V. Pandey
DevopsInternational B.V, Amsterdam, The Netherlands
e-mail: vikpande@devopsinternational.nl

G. Bapuji
Women in Crisis Response LLC, Cambridge, MA, USA
e-mail: godhabapuji@wicr.org

M. Petersen
Kuehne Logistics University, Hamburg, Germany
e-mail: moritz.petersen@the-klu.org

B. Hobson
Circular & Sustainable Supply Chain Advisor, New York, NY, USA
e-mail: bettinablouson@gmail.com

W. Lehmacher
Industrial Innovation Partners, Anchor Group, Geneva, Switzerland
e-mail: w.lehmacher@gmail.com

A. Turos
7 Chapters of Circularity, The Hague, The Netherlands
e-mail: attila@7chaptersofcircularity.com

1 Introduction: Circular Economy for Resource Efficiency

1.1 *A Resource Strained Planet*

The pull on the planet's carrying capacity has been increasingly strained since the Industrial Revolution sparked the development of modern linear production practices. In the current globalising linear economy or production model—raw materials are extracted from resource dense countries, transported to manufacturers, and processed into various products. The finished goods then get shipped, maybe a great distance, to where they are used, discarded at their end-of-life, and eventually replaced by newer iterations. This has recently been amplified with the rise of e-commerce as we turn towards an increasingly global, digital economy. In our modern economy, resource throughput is enormous, highly international, and only recovered to a small degree (OECD 2019).

The long-term consequences of this global linear production model are that both the planet's source function (resource extraction) and sink functions (emissions to water, air, and soil) have multiplied (Daly 1991).

Environmental policies arising from the 1940s and accelerating from the 1970s and onwards have sought to remedy these still more felt and gradually recognised negative environmental effects, including climate change. With the expected global population growth and increase in consumption per capita following the rapid and current rise of the middle class in the emerging economies, this trend is estimated to continue (Ellen MacArthur Foundation 2013). However, we can now also see corrective mechanisms in the advanced economies, where for example the energy consumption per capita is declining (Our World in Data 2019), the circular economy being one of these corrective mechanisms.

The quest to achieve a more resource-efficient economy by changing to more sustainable production and consumption patterns through green and circular innovations will continue. It is positive that this condition is increasingly recognised and addressed by both policymakers and businesses: Most recently with the EU Circular Economy Action Plan (European Commission 2020a, b) "*Scaling up the circular economy from front-runners to the mainstream economic players will make a decisive contribution to achieving climate neutrality by 2050 and decoupling economic growth from resource use, while ensuring the long-term competitiveness of the EU and leaving no one behind*".

1.2 *Circular Economy for a Resource-Efficient Economy*

Globally, the circular economy concept is increasingly seen as a way forward to achieve the necessary transformation into a resource-efficient economy. While circular thinking is not new and has for some time formed part of environmental research and policymaking, for example Club of Rome from the 1970s (Club of

Rome 2021), there are several new features to the circular economy agenda. The circular economy is resource preserving and regenerative by design, and with as many closed loops as possible. There is new attention to the systematic, intelligent use of resources, including design for recycling, whereas recycling hitherto only has taken place without interfering with existing business practices. With the rise of circular economy policies, such as the high recycling targets and Extended Producer Responsibility schemes central to the EU Circular Economy Action Plans (European Commission 2015) and (European Commission 2020a, b) as well as a range of new circular standards, an increasing number of producers are experiencing stronger incentives to undertake research and design for recycling. Markets are responding positively, and circular business models are on the rise. Still, the challenge of developing profitable high-value products out of all residues (upcycling) is immense. Also, the development of new circular business models, including models for efficient sharing, exchange, and maintenance of resources, is only emerging. Lacking knowledge about design and recycling as well as traceability of materials and products and limited circular standards hampers this development. While recycling was targeted by policymaking early, implementation was only seen in the form of the easy stand-alone recycling model that did not interfere with established production methods and business models. The current circular economy agenda applies a very different disruptive approach that questions many established business practices and sources of competitiveness.

Fundamentally, the idea of the circular economy is to redesign usage that leads to less waste and more value so that at the systemic level we achieve a near zero-waste economy.

One reason why the circular economy agenda is on the rise is the recent increase in attention to the 'source' side; in other words, the economic pressure from rising resource prices and expected shortcomings in vital minerals, especially for the important digital industry (de Groot et al. 2012) and for heavy industries, like the maritime sector. In the past, the discovery of new resource deposits and advances in mining have generally led to a decline in resource prices. Resource prices for metals, minerals, fuels, fish, timber, and biomass generally decreased until 1998 (an overall decrease of 55% in real prices during 1980–1998), after which they have been steadily increasing, on average real prices increased by more than 300% between 1998 and 2011 (European Commission 2012).

While sometimes used interchangeably, sustainability and a circular economy are different agendas. Sustainable development targets at a very general level the overall societal ability to sustain itself; that is, to maintain the human- and biosystems within the carrying capacity of the planet in the long run. Aligning social, economic, and environmental concerns are at the heart of the sustainable development agenda. The circular economy is a sub agenda targeting the efficient use and recovery of resources. It represents a novel vision for how we may achieve a resource-efficient and profitable modern global economy. *"The intentional design of a system is what separates circularity from sustainability"* (U.S. Chamber of Commerce Foundation 2020).

1.3   Circularity's Economic Potential and the Maritime Industry

The climate agenda and the transition towards a global circular economy may, if wisely addressed, represent a business opportunity for many industries, including the maritime sector.

By 2030 the linear economy's inability to deal with the growing demand for resources will result in a large gap between supply and demand for constrained natural resources (Lacy and Rutqvist 2015). This is estimated to translate into USD4.5 trillion of lost growth by 2030 and growing to USD25 trillion by 2050 (Lacy and Rutqvist 2015).

Executive Vice-President for the European Green Deal, Frans Timmermans, said: *"To achieve climate-neutrality by 2050, to preserve our natural environment, and to strengthen our economic competitiveness, requires a fully circular economy. Today, our economy is still mostly linear, with only 12% of secondary materials and resources being brought back into the economy. Many products break down too easily, cannot be reused, repaired, or recycled, or are made for single use only. There is a huge potential to be exploited both for businesses and consumers"* (European Commission 2020a, b).

The European Commission estimates that the circular economy promises savings for EU businesses and the creation of hundred of thousands of jobs while reducing the EU's carbon emissions (European Commission 2015).

Mainstreaming circular supply chains, leveraging recovery and recycling, designing and manufacturing long-lasting and recyclable products, sharing idle assets, and servicing products are core features for realising the benefits. The circular economy will not remove but will reduce waste, creating new business opportunities.

For the maritime sector with many long-lasting products based mainly on steel, it is vital today to plan for when these products have reached their end of use, when resources may be scarce. With maritime and other heavy industries heavily dependent on steel, recycling and reuse of steel are critical to sustaining maritime and other heavy industries long term. Today, recycling can mean a reduction in quality of the materials (downcycling). For example, steel scrap often contaminated with copper from wires and tin from coatings is problematic for reusing the steel and can, for example, cause cracks during processing (ChemistryViews.org 2017). However, some initiatives focus on preserving the quality of materials when ships are being recycled. An example is described by the World Economic Forum: *"Maersk has created a digital twin of their latest container ships down to the smallest bolt. Through this, the company will ultimately know how much and what material is being used in their fleet ... a clear systemic view on which parts and materials can be reused, remanufactured, upcycled or continue to stay in the circular flow of shipbuilding"* (Schmid and Ritzrau 2018).

Maersk Decom is another maritime circularity example. The company are dismantling, and recycling materials used by the offshore energy industry. It is designing recycling and waste management routes that optimise the resource yields of the circulating products and waste fractions (Maersk Decom 2019).

2   Opportunities for Circularity in the Maritime Industry

The maritime industry is a cornerstone of global economic development. Although it is not known as an industry that is leading the transition to a circular economy, several semi-circular business models have been in place in the maritime industry for decades as they offer good business sense, such as container logistics, predictive maintenance, and ship demolition. For the industry to harvest the business and environmental benefits from the circular economy concept we are seeing initiatives and projects emerge throughout the industry that could lead to a higher degree of circularity.

The following section is based on interviews conducted with experts from shipbuilding, shipping companies, ports, and international maritime organisations to inquire about the state of play on maritime circularity and identify opportunities for improvement. In this section, we introduce some of the current initiatives, further opportunities, and the role of digitalisation. We have used the five circular business models from the Circular Economy Handbook to structure our findings (Lacy et al. 2020)—circular inputs, sharing economy and industrial platforms, product as a service, product use extension, and resource recovery.

2.1   Current Initiatives: Circular Inputs

In a circular economy, renewable, recycled, or highly recyclable inputs are used in the production processes, enabling partial or total elimination of waste and pollution (Lacy et al. 2020). In the maritime industry, such circular inputs are renewable resources like wind and solar energy, and renewable human-made materials like steel, zinc, and copper, that can be recycled without a substantial loss of quality or physical properties. It is important to maintain the materials' quality level during reuse by categorising them according to their quality, for instance, by designating steel as high or low-quality steel.

Using renewable energy is relatively easy to implement in ports. More and more terminals are electrifying their cranes, straddle carriers, and other equipment. In shipping, most energy used must be produced onboard the ship, usually by burning fossil fuel. Wind propulsion for ships is being looked into to replace a share of the fossil-fuel-based energy used to power ships (Lind et al. 2021c). Examples of such technologies being explored are large kites and airfoils.

Ballini (2020) describes an example in the Copenhagen Malmö Port where four elements of ship-waste (organic solid waste, black and grey water (sewage), and port waste management), biogas plant and shore-to-ship power supply are used to set up a closed-loop model. The port authority will take care of waste management from cruise ships and use the waste in a port-owned biogas plant, which produces clean electricity from ship waste and to some extent contributes to port energy self sufficiency. Finally, the resultant clean electricity is consumed in port for shore supply to ships or other purposes like energy for port buildings. Based on net present value (NPV) calculations, the recovery of investment is achieved in the seventh year.

2.2   Current Initiatives: Sharing economy Concept and Industrial Platforms

The sharing economy concept emphasises the intelligent use of idle assets by maximising the sharing of assets between organisations or individuals. This entails that the utilisation rates of products, assets or productive activities are optimised through shared ownership or access (Lacy et al. 2020; Watson et al. 2021).

This sharing is typically enabled by digital technologies, particularly when it comes to establishing a professional sharing economy between companies. Today, sharing economy industrial platforms have not been developed systematically for industries. So, this is only an emerging trend in the circular economy representing a novel business model. The focus of maritime informatics on data sharing and data analytics can support the higher utilisation of assets and the coordination of shared resources (Lind et al. 2020b),

A Sharing Economy Platform enables owners to maximise how assets are used (shared) across a community while providing customers with affordable and convenient access to products and services.

In the maritime sector, there are already many examples of the sharing economy, such as the tugboats, and terminals, whose use needs to be coordinated (Lind et al. 2021a). Perhaps, when more terminals become autonomous, we will even see the sharing of core equipment like straddle carriers.

The following illustration (Fig. 1) shows how the use of an autonomous sharing platform, reduces barriers to efficient container leasing and thereby increases the usage rate per container.

Such a registry of all containers' actual and estimated position can also be used by the marine industry's business intelligence tools to optimise plans for empty container repositioning, thereby increasing the average utilisation rate of containers. To protect confidential business information the actual/estimated position of the container should be anonymised, and access controlled by the data owner.

Another example, to increase the utilisation of products in the tramp shipping market, is the use of a digital sharing platform and business intelligence, to enable better matching between cargo and ships' destinations to reduce the number of ships lying idle.

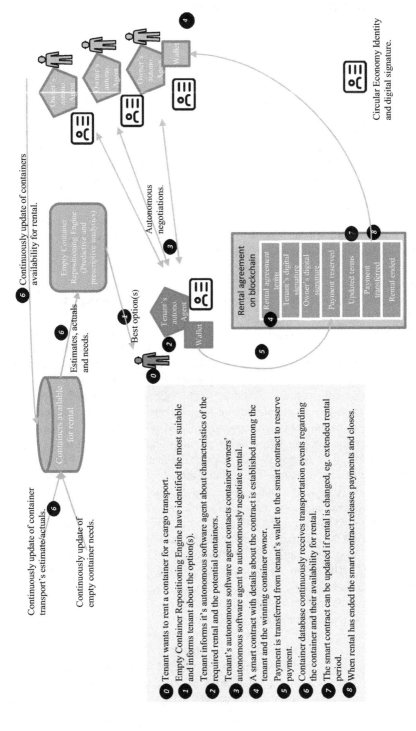

Fig. 1 Distributed Autonomous Software Agents reduce barriers to container sharing

2.3   Current Initiatives: Product as a Service

There are three categories of service delivery (Tukker 2020):

- Product-oriented where the focus is on buying a product that gives you the desired outcome. In such cases, the responsibility and ownership of the product, including its end-of-life handling, are typically transferred linearly to the client (You own your car).
- Use-oriented where the focus is still around the product, but where the product is owned by the provider and is made available to the client (Car sharing or hiring).
- Outcome-oriented where the provider delivers an agreed outcome to the client, without a predetermined product involved (You just want to be transported to a specific place).

In the use-oriented and the outcome-oriented model, the provider retains ownership of a product and sells its benefits on a service basis while remaining responsible for the good's ongoing maintenance and treatment at the end of use.

In the maritime sector, the container has since the 1960s been an example of the product as a service (Watson et al. 2017; Lind et al. 2020a). Here, the container's ownership stays with the carrier, while the shipper uses it to transport cargo and returns the container to the carrier.

The product as a service approach places the incentive for product durability and upgrading on the provider, shifting focus from volume to performance. As the provider remains the product-owner, it enables some attractive models where the provider has an economic interest in making the product circular.

The provider retains control of products and materials and is therefore in better control of the supply of essential material for future products. The provider saves material costs, protects themselves against material price shocks, and can hedge against material scarcity issues (See the previous example regarding the scarcity of steel (Sect. 1.3) and other materials critical for the maritime sector). The provider benefits from continued customer contact, and therefore gets insights into how their products are used. The provider also gains access to potential untapped opportunities for businesses, for example, a new remanufacturing/refurbishment market. Materials that are not required by the provider allows other refurbishing or reuse facilities who may be able to use the material. For example, the existing market for old containers.

There are, however, some new challenges. Products must be designed for remanufacturing. The easier the product can be taken apart, the easier it can be remanufactured. For example, fastening methods on maritime equipment should be chosen so that parts can be easily replaced or fixed. Detailed descriptions of the materials used in the construction of a ship and cargo handling equipment become essential. Likewise, it requires new considerations of materials to use as it will be in the provider's interest to select materials for durability.

Another challenge is that manufacturers need to find ways to get the material back for remanufacturing. The reverse value chain will be a new logistic capability. The issue is how to make it economically attractive throughout the value chain to get the used materials back to the original provider. The first-mile logistic, getting an end-of-use product from the consumer back to the first logistic collection point, is a new challenge for the logistics industry. Although outside the scope of this chapter, it is worth mentioning that the materials that in a circular economy do not end up at a local landfill as waste, must be transported to a place for remanufacturing, refurbishment, or recycling. This requires logistics and potentially more cargo for the maritime sector.

The provider now has a responsibility and an economic incentive for safer disposal mechanisms, a responsibility that previously was on the end-user, often without a financial incentive.

2.4 Current Initiatives: Product Use Extension

In a circular economy, a product's use in its intended application is purposefully extended through design considerations, repairs, component reconditioning, upgrades, and resale on secondary markets (Lacy et al. 2020).

This generally is in line with how the maritime sector for a long time has managed its business. With product life cycles that last several decades, the marine industry has established experience in middle-of-life maintenance and services, and maritime has developed secondary markets for ships and equipment used on them. The transition to this aspect of circularity is, therefore, a natural extension of the maritime business-as-usual. An example is Wärtsilä, the technology company producing power, nautical and other ship systems in the maritime and energy markets, Wärtsilä also extends the lifetime of worn-out equipment to their full functionality so that a vessel's license to operate, and revenue potential remains, while, at the same time, operational expenditures and impact to the environment are reduced.

Product Use Extension is applied during or at the end of a product's first use. An example is the retrofitting of a ship's bulbous bow to optimise a ship's operational slow steaming profile.

Another example is the emergence of predictive maintenance platforms for engines and other critical ship systems. Using data acquired from sensors and data transmitted ashore via satellite, enables analysis that can assess a component's condition in real-time, and propose maintenance procedures and shore side support as and when necessary. This extends a system's lifetime, reduces risks, and saves operational expenditures.

The use of data and digital tools to increase efficiency and automation in ports is another example of product use extension. This enables the infrastructures to be idle as little as possible, thereby ensuring higher capital productivity for port operations (Watson et al. 2021).

Also, Maersk is trialling a battery system onboard its container ships. This will allow the auxiliary engines to be operated at optimum speed, thereby reducing maintenance (Maersk 2019).

A final development related to spare parts is to use additive manufacturing technologies (3D printing) on a vessel to produce only those spare parts that are needed. While these technologies still have a long way to go concerning performance, these projects illustrate the opportunity to cut back on materials through not-producing unnecessary spare parts.

Beyond ships, old shipping containers are sometimes upcycled and used for housing or other storage purposes. Such product use extensions contribute to significant material resource savings and value savings in cost, labour, and energy.

2.5 Current Initiatives: Resource Recovery

The value of embedded materials or energy from agricultural and industrial goods is captured through collection, aggregation, and processing at the end of a product's use through recycling, upcycling, or downcycling infrastructures and practices (Lacy et al. 2020).

Resource recovery focuses on the end stages of the value chain, namely the recovery of materials and resources from products at the end of use that are no longer functional in their current application.

The maritime industry has experience from the demolition of ships. However, the current demolition practice often results in the quality of the materials being degraded. In a circular economy, the recovered resource is used in a way that maintains its highest possible value for the longest time. Separating high and low-grade steel, copper wiring, aluminium, insulation materials, zinc, hazardous materials, and waste. Based on the sorting, it will be possible to reuse nearly all materials at their existing quality for new ships, thus making dangerous and polluting scrapping a thing of the past.

This lowers the demand for iron ore mining, reduces energy use in, for example, the steelmaking process, and ensures the maritime sector has a predictable and consistent future flow of materials for shipbuilding. The marine industry thereby controls such material flow, not the mining industry. An example is Wärtsilä's end-of-life ship propellers being used in casting new propellers.

Global structured implementation of maritime circular material passports means that ships, gantry cranes, straddle carriers, etc., that have reached the end of their effective or economic service lives can be considered material banks waiting for "maritime mining". The value of an end-of-life ship will be higher when it has up-to-date maritime circular material passports, for which digitalisation provides an essential component (see the framework for digital circular material passports in Sect. 4.7). In 2012, Maersk estimated a 10% higher price for recycling of vessels (Sterling 2012); we have no recent data to confirm this forecast.

3 Digitalising Maritime Circularity

3.1 The Need for a Coherent Structure that Connects all Stakeholders

The last few decades growth of manufacturing and other industries has ended up creating a multitude of physical products and materials. Most of these, after their use, are either not registered digitally or not tracked in a digitised way. Due to this trend, industries are not able to properly know about the availability, type, quality, or quantity of resource flows that are available to be reused or recycled.

For those items that are tracked, there are multiple systems or digital solutions, each of which has its format or structure for storing and saving information about products in use, their life length, and availability for reuse. This creates siloes of information and deters the possibility of data exchanges, hence, not promoting a coherent circular economy to its optimum.

Digitalisation and interoperability are critical for realising a coherent digital structure that connects all stakeholders. Currently, most circular economy initiatives are individual projects focused on materials and resources. However, to scale these solutions globally and across industries, we need to build coherent digital foundations to support attractive global circularity business models and accelerate the journey towards circularity.

Digital technologies and data exchange drive a significant part of the transformation to the circular economy (Lacy et al. 2020). We will focus on why a shared digital backbone for the circular economy is a prerequisite for realising an efficient circular economy across geographies and industries. We expect the realisation of such a digital backbone to be the most impactful activity towards the circular economy. Both in terms of enabling more economically viable circular business models as well as accelerating the environmental impact of the circular economy.

Notably, we see that such digital foundations for the circular economy can be based on well-known and well-performing technologies. Hence, there is no need to wait for maturation of information technologies to realise the digital backbone; they are already available.

3.2 A Shared Digital Foundation for the Circular Economy

In the linear economy, companies primarily focus on the immediate next business partner; however, an essential criterion for scaling an interrelated value chain business model like the circular economy is digital collaboration and standardisation throughout the business ecosystem (Lind et al. 2021b).

Companies are working across industries and materials used in a product in one industry can be reused in other industries. In the circular economy context, you cannot treat the maritime industry or any other industry in isolation; it must be an integrated part of the global circular economy. The implementation of activities that globally can support the shipping industry's transition to maritime circularity will require cross-regional cooperation among stakeholders within the industry and with other industries.

Single focused digitalisation is therefore not sufficient. Accelerating digital circular economy innovations requires the realisation of a shared digital backbone for the circular economy—just like the Internet exponentially accelerated the global digital innovation. Based on historic digital platform performance and business digitalisation benefits an organisation would gain an average of a 20–40% improvement on their circularity business goals by leveraging a digital circular economy backbone (Giemzo et al. 2020).

A digital circular economy backbone ensures the circular economy functions seamlessly on a global as well as on a regional and cross-industry scale, enabling interoperable business models, easy visibility, and exchange of used materials globally and between industries. It will reduce cost, time, and risk for realising digital circular economy solutions. In doing so, it accelerates the realisation of the circular economy and allows more circular business models to be commercially and environmentally viable.

4 Towards a Digital Foundation Framework for a Circular Economy

Figure 2 illustrates a potential framework for a digital circular economy backbone (Circular Economy Internet 2020). It is designed according to the principles of a digital global public good that is commercially, competitively, and politically neutral, while allowing innovative and differentiating business models to be realised.

In the following sections, the framework's properties are elaborated on and used to illustrate the potential of a digital circular economy backbone. The framework is an application of the maritime digital stack as elaborated by Watson et al. (2021).

4.1 Property #1: Modularity

The components in the digital circular economy backbone will be modular, in the sense that every component will work independently as a feature and together with other components to complete the digital backbone for the circular economy. An example is the material pool (described in Sect. 4.7), which would be used to store information about the material. It could also be integrated into other modules and external solutions via appropriate Application Programming Interfaces (APIs) to add more value than just being a system of record. Standardisation of digital data exchange is critical for modularity.

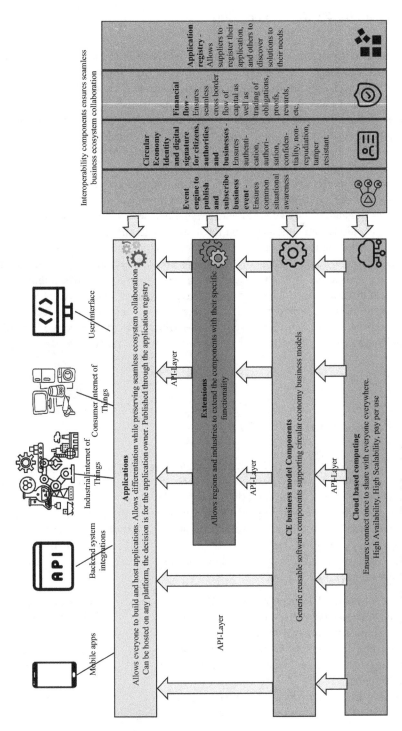

Fig. 2 A framework for a Circular Economy digital foundation

4.2   Property #2: Interoperability

An essential criterion for a circular economy backbone is to facilitate digital eco-system many-to-many interoperability (Becha et al. 2021) to reduce barriers, cost, risk, and resources for citizens, businesses, and governments to participate in global circular economy value chains.

In Fig. 2, the horizontal cloud layer shown in blue and vertical components shown in purple support the connected circular economy by enabling efficient digital interoperability throughout global value chains. Examples of such interoperability components are an event engine allowing everyone in the value chain to publish and subscribe to business events ensuring a common situational awareness. Circular Economy Identity and digital signature (CEID) is a global common digital identity and digital signature for citizens, authorities, and businesses that ensure authentica-tion, authorisation, confidentiality, non-repudiation, and tamper resistance through-out global value chains. The financial flow enables an interoperable infrastructure for the flow of money and trading of obligations, proofs, rewards, etc. It makes a company's realisation of such a business model simpler. It allows obligations, proofs, and rewards to be traded across industries, products, and materials.

Interoperability must be designed to work seamlessly with the linear economy, so, for example, the CEID can be used together with the World Economic Forum's Global Trade Identity (Hvid Jensen and Hewett 2019; Lind et al. 2021b).

4.3   Property #3: Generic Digital Support of Circular Economy Business Models

The green layer shown in Fig. 2 indicates components implementing generic digital support of circular economy business models (such as those described in Sect. 2). This will be the shared digital toolbox supporting the circular economy that reduces cost, time, and risk in realising digital circular economy business models, as it will be developed based on modularity, reusability, and interoperability principles. This generic digital support will eventually be the basis for creating standards for the circular economy. Examples of shared components in such a toolbox are (Circular Economy Internet 2020):

- Circular Material Passport Engine (CMPE)—A generic component that supports digital material passports. The maritime industry, the car industry, the white goods industry, etc. will create extensions for their specific needs. Individual companies can then make their application on top of the extensions, or the industry can create generic applications. See Fig. 3 for a maritime implementation.
- The Industrial Sharing Economy (SE)—A generic digital engine that supports the industrial sharing economy. A generic digital engine is conceived as the

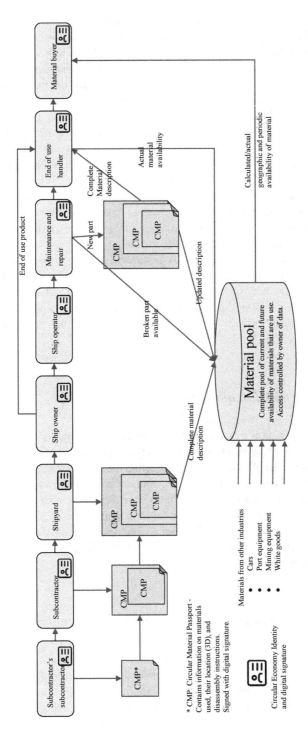

Fig. 3 Information flow for circular material passport and the material pool

underlying common logic that supports an interoperable industrial sharing mechanism. A shared engine with ready-made tools makes it easier to share cross-industrial assets that would otherwise be underused. It is a way to increase access to goods and services without the need for individual ownership. In Fig. 1 that illustrates a digital container sharing framework the shared components (the green layer in Fig. 2) would be how the autonomous agent negotiates, the registration of the agreement, and the financial flow. Whereas the actual asset identification and description, as well as the renting conditions, would be separate per industry and application (the red and yellow layers).

- The proof provider (PP)—Proofing resources utilised, or waste generated has been recycled, refactored, etc.
- Exterior packaging (EP)—An aggregated database with information on how packaging can be reused. One shared place to find the information provided by individual solutions, without jeopardising the individual solution's business model. It ensures a global interoperable format.
- Materials Marketplace/Pool (MM)—A generic digital engine for an online materials exchange platform. Aligning with circular economy principles, the platform facilitates keeping materials and products out of the landfill and in use. A Material Marketplace/Pool will not only reduce waste management expenditure but also provide the means for local businesses to advertise and bid for surpluses (see Fig. 3 for a maritime implementation).

4.4 Property #4: Extendibility

The Extension layer shown in red in Fig. 2 indicates that industries and regions can broaden the generic components according to their specific needs. For the maritime sector, it will, for example, be necessary to define maritime extensions to a circular material passport to describe ships, cranes, containers, etc. in a way that is interoperable across all actors within the maritime sector as well as with other industries. Some of the key concepts to be captured under this are semantics, taxonomy, data structures and data exchange rules. The Hong Kong International Convention for the Safe and Environmentally Sound Recycling of Ships (Hong Kong 2009) would be digitally implemented in this layer.

4.5 Property #5: Support Differentiation and Innovation

The backbone must be designed as an open software platform, allowing innovators and companies worldwide to realise individual value-adding and differentiating but still interoperable applications on top. The application layer shown in yellow in Fig. 2 and the application registry shown vertically in purple enable innovation and differentiation.

The application registry allows providers to register their application, and others to discover solutions to their needs. Making all digital circular economy applications globally available and interoperable like how a mobile app is available globally via internet portals such as Apple's app store.

This layer enables a build once used everywhere internet-like paradigm where any solutions are immediately available globally, extending the commercial potential and the speed of global realisation of the best digital circular economy solutions.

4.6 Property #6: A Global Public Good

To be globally acceptable the digital backbone must be designed and governed as a global public good while enabling businesses to realise innovative value-adding solutions and differentiating business models.

The digital backbone must be politically, commercially, and competitively neutral. This means that each jurisdiction decides how to handle available information according to national policy frameworks, that no one person, company, organisation, or government controls the digital backbone, and that each country's required investment is insignificant, supporting developing countries, and small and medium business participation.

Data must be controlled by the owner of the data, which also eliminates the monopolisation of digital circular economy concepts. Due to network effects, we have seen how the digital platform concept can give rise to monopolies. Having essential data, business process and logic, transaction, and trust as shared components that are politically, competitively, and commercially neutral, protects the circular economy concepts against monopolisation, while still benefiting from the digital ecosystem collaboration and network effect.

The digital backbone must have a business model that makes it sustainable as a business.

4.7 Detailing the Circular Material Passport and the Material Pool

To illustrate the requirement for extendable components (the green layer in Fig. 2) that can be reused across industries and regions, this section details two components that often are used together and will be critical for efficient maritime circularity; the Circular Material Passport and the Material Pool (Fig. 3), description is based on (Circular Economy Internet 2020). Both are critical digital components to facilitate a circular material system where materials are reused in their existing quality while enabling a good business case for everyone involved.

The circular material passport gives a detailed understanding of what individual products are made of when they are made, and by whom. It will contain a distributed database, including security that ensures integrity and that the data owner controls access to data. The circular material passport ensures global availability of detailed and complete information about materials used in the product, their location, how to disassemble and recycle a product, irrespective of how the maritime business environment develops in 20–30 years.

The digital backbone's "interoperability by design" is crucial as many producers and suppliers have myriad upstream and downstream partners within several industries. This means that a digital integration through a connect-once-to-share-with-everyone backbone instead of one-to-one integrations is the only viable approach.

The circular material passport will feed the global material pool. The global circular material pool gives a complete global overview of the future availability of materials that are currently in use, whether it is ships, gantry cranes, white goods, cars, etc. The circular material pool holds the possibility for the owner of a product to announce the expected end of use cycle. It is a marketplace for urban/maritime mining of materials that can be adjusted by regional and industrial requirements.

Most materials can be used almost endlessly as long as they are kept pure, as long as they are designed for disassembly and reuse and as long as we have tracking systems in place that allow us to identify what they are once they have passed through their first use cycle. Through applying circular design principles, municipalities, regions, countries, and companies (including ports, terminals, ship owners) could almost turn their entire stock of in-use materials into a competitive asset, made available through a global material pool and described on their circular material passport.

The generic circular material passport and material pool can be extended for any industry including the maritime industry while preserving the global cross-industrial interoperability. Supporting a good business case for producers of maritime equipment (ships, cranes, etc.), and the other actors along the value chain.

A maritime circular material passport must be prepared for efficient API-based retrospective updates of existing maritime equipment. In many cases, detailed information about the materials used to build maritime equipment already exist in digital format. It just must be transferred to the maritime circular material passport. This means that the maritime sector does not have to wait until the end of life for future new buildings to harvest the benefits from circular material passports and material pool. The benefit harvesting can start immediately when retrospective data of existing assets has been uploaded to the maritime equipment's material passport.

The digital backbone will hold generic interoperable (blue and purple layers in Fig. 2) components supporting digital circular material passports and circular material pool (green layer in Fig. 2). The maritime industry should create extensions needed to support the maritime industry (red layer in Fig. 2). This can for example be the Hong Kong Convention. The individual actors in the maritime industry may then create their value-adding and differentiating applications on top of the maritime industry's extended components (yellow layer in Fig. 2). The digital backbone interoperability by design allows seamless and secure access to all the partners in their business ecosystem in a connect-once-to-share-with-everyone-everywhere scenario.

5   Conclusion

The circular economy offers new principles of doing business in a systematic resource preserving way that may turn into good business cases, while also reducing our environmental impacts substantially. The maritime sector is well prepared for adopting these principles, not least because the industry already has an ever-increasing amount of its physical infrastructures described by digital means and has several semi-circular business models implemented.

The circular economy is changing the rules and practices of business in many important ways. However, those first successfully adopting circular economy principles are likely to be more competitive, as we have often seen when companies adopt other new business models (platform business, containerised logistics, social media, etc.)

While the International Maritime Organization (IMO) emissions goals only address one-third of the potential emission from the maritime industry, the circular economy addresses the remainder (CGR 2019), meaning that maritime circularity will have a bigger impact on the world than the IMO's current goals.

Focused and responsible digitalisation of the circular economy will be important to accelerate the realisation of its economic and environmental potentials. A shared interoperable digital backbone for the circular economy will add substantially to the digital benefits, accelerate the environmental impacts, and make more circular economy business models attractive.

Acknowledgements We are grateful to Jan Hoffmann, Chief, Trade Logistics Branch, DTL at UNCTAD; Professor Jean-Paul Rodrigue, Hofstra University, USA; Vesa Marttinen, Managing Director, Wärtsilä; Wolfgang Lehmacher, Supply chain and Technology Strategies; who have provided their insights on the maritime industry and the circular economy.

References

Ballini F (2020) Sustainability and circular economy approach in ports, 7 Oct 2020. https://unece. org/fileadmin/DAM/trans/doc/2020/sc3/04._CE_in_Ports_context_-__WMU_Ballini_F_ UNECE.pdf

Becha H, Schroeder M, Voorspuij J, Frazier T, Lind M (2021) Global data exchange standards: the basis for future smart container digital services. In: Lind M, Michaelides M, Ward R, Watson RT (eds) Maritime informatics. Springer, Heidelberg

CGR (2019) The Platform for Accelerating the Circular Economy (PACE). The Circularity Gap Report. https://shiftingparadigms.nl/wp-content/uploads/2019/01/CGR-2.0-report-final-reprint-web-20190326.pdf

ChemistryViews.org (2017) Copper as a growing problem for steel recycling. https://www.chemistryviews.org/details/news/10527707/Copper_as_a_Growing_Problem_for_Steel_Recycling.html

Circular Economy Internet (2020) https://circulareconomyinternet.com/

Club of Rome (2021) The Club of Rome was created to address the multiple crises facing humanity and the planet. https://www.clubofrome.org/

Daly HE (1991) Steady-state economics, 2nd edn. Island Press, Washington, DC. isbn:978-1559630726

de Groot HLF, Rademaekers K et al (2012) Mapping resource prices: the past and the future, 25 Oct 2012. https://ec.europa.eu/environment/enveco/resource_efficiency/pdf/studies/summary_mapping_resource_prices.pdf

Ellen MacArthur Foundation (2013) Towards the circular economy. Towards the Circular Economy. https://doi.org/10.1162/108819806775545321

European Commission (2012) Mapping resource prices: the past and the future https://ec.europa.eu/environment/enveco/resource_efficiency/pdf/studies/summary_mapping_resource_prices.pdf

European Commission (2015) Circular economy closing the loop. https://ec.europa.eu/commission/sites/beta-political/files/circular-economy-factsheet-general_en.pdf

European Commission (2020a) Changing how we produce and consume: new circular economy action plan shows the way to a climate-neutral, competitive economy of empowered consumers. https://ec.europa.eu/commission/presscorner/detail/en/ip_20_420

European Commission (2020b) EU circular economy action plan. https://ec.europa.eu/environment/circular-economy/

Giemzo J, Gu M, Kaplan J, Vinter L (2020) How CIOs and CTOs can accelerate digital transformations through cloud platforms, 15 Sept 2020. https://www.mckinsey.com/business-functions/mckinsey-digital/our-insights/how-cios-and-ctos-can-accelerate-digital-transformations-through-cloud-platforms#-

Hong Kong (2009) Hong Kong international convention for the safe and environmentally sound recycling of ships. https://mst.dk/media/93669/hong-kong-konventionen.pdf

Hvid Jensen H, Hewett N (2019) Inclusive deployment of blockchain for supply chains part 2—trustworthy verification of digital identities, 1 Sept 2019. https://www.weforum.org/whitepapers/inclusive-deployment-of-blockchain-for-supply-chains-part-2-trustworthy-verification-of-digital-identities

Lacy P, Rutqvist J (2015) Waste to wealth: the circular economy advantage. Springer, Cham

Lacy P, Long J, Spindler W (2020) The circular economy handbook: realizing the circular advantage. Palgrave Macmillan, London

Lind M, Becha H, Simha A, Bottin F, Larsen SE (2020a) Digital containerisation. Smart Maritime Network, 18 June 2020. https://smartmaritimenetwork.com/wp-content/uploads/2020/06/Information-transparency-through-standardised-messaging-and-interfacing.pdf

Lind M, Watson R, Hoffmann J, Ward R, Michaelides M (2020b) Maritime Informatics: an emerging discipline for a digitally connected efficient, sustainable and resilient industry, Article No. 59 [UNCTAD Transport and Trade Facilitation Newsletter N°87—Third Quarter 2020]. https://unctad.org/en/pages/newsdetails.aspx?OriginalVersionID=2456

Lind M, Ward R, Watson RT, Haraldson S, Zerem A, Paulsen S (2021a) Decision support for port visits. In: Lind M, Michaelides M, Ward R, Watson RT (eds) Maritime informatics. Springer, Heidelberg

Lind M, Ward R, Hvid Jensen H, Chua CP, Simha A, Karlsson J, Göthberg L, Penttinen T, Theodosiou DP (2021b) The future of shipping—collaboration through digital data sharing. In: Lind M, Michaelides M, Ward R, Watson RT (eds) Maritime informatics. Springer, Heidelberg

Lind M, Haraldson S, Carson-Jackson J, Gardeichik J, Singh S, Zuesongdham P, Morton R, Pettersson S, Pernia O, Larsen SE (2021c) Ports as multidimensional hubs. In: Lind M, Michaelides M, Ward R, Watson RT (eds) Maritime informatics: additional perspectives and applications. Springer, Heidelberg

Maersk (2019) Maersk to pilot a battery system to improve power production https://www.maersk. com/news/articles/2019/11/06/maersk-to-pilot-a-battery-system-to-improve-power-production

Maersk Decom (2019) Maersk Decom. Recycling & Waste Management Solutions, https://www. maerskdecom.com/wp-content/uploads/2019/12/Maersk-Decom-recycling-and-waste-manage ment-27122019.pdf

OECD (2019) Global material resources outlook to 2060: economic drivers and environmental consequences. OECD, Paris. https://doi.org/10.1787/9789264307452-en

Our World in Data (2019) Energy use per person. https://ourworldindata.org/grapher/per-capita-energy-use

Schmid D, Ritzrau W (2018) Why the circular economy must link up the whole supply chain. https://www.weforum.org/agenda/2018/09/why-the-circular-economy-needs-to-link-up-the-whole-supply-chain/

Sterling J (2012) Cradle to cradle passport—towards a new industry standard in ship building https://www.oecd.org/sti/ind/48354596.pdf

Tukker A (2020) Business value in a circular economy episode 2, https://courses.edx.org/courses/course-v1:Delftx+CircularX+1T2020a/course/

US Chamber of Commerce Foundation (2020) Circularity vs. sustainability, https://www. uschamberfoundation.org/circular-economy-toolbox/about-circularity/circularity-vs-sustainability

Watson RT, Lind M, Haraldson S (2017) Physical and digital innovation in shipping: seeding, standardizing, and sequencing. Paper presented at the Hawaii International Conference on Systems Science 2017

Watson RT, Lind M, Delmeire N, Liesa F (2021) Shipping: a self-organising ecosystem. In: Lind M, Michaelides M, Ward R, Watson RT (eds) Maritime informatics. Springer, Heidelberg

Ports as Multidimensional Hubs

Mikael Lind ⓘ, **Sandra Haraldson** ⓘ, **Jillian Carson-Jackson** ⓘ,
Jan Gardeitchik ⓘ, **Sukhjit Singh** ⓘ, **Phanthian Zuesongdham** ⓘ,
Richard Morton ⓘ, **Stefan Pettersson** ⓘ, **Oscar Pernia** ⓘ, and
Steen Erik Larsen ⓘ

M. Lind (✉) · S. Pettersson
Research Institutes of Sweden (RISE), Chalmers University of Technology, Gothenburg,
Sweden
e-mail: mikael@realsearchers.com; stefan.pettersson@ri.se

S. Haraldson
Research Institutes of Sweden (RISE), Gothenburg, Sweden
e-mail: sandra@realsearchers.com

J. Carson-Jackson
The Nautical Institute, London, UK
e-mail: jillian@jcjconsulting.net

J. Gardeitchik
Yaquina Consulting & Management, Rotterdam, The Netherlands
e-mail: jan@yaquina.nl

S. Singh
The University of Trinidad and Tobag, Chaguaramas, Trinidad and Tobago
e-mail: sukhjit.singh@utt.edu.tt

P. Zuesongdham
Hamburg Port Authority, Hamburg, Germany
e-mail: Phanthian.Zuesongdham@hpa.hamburg.de

R. Morton
International Port Community Systems Association, Felixstowe, UK
e-mail: Richard.morton@ipcsa.international

O. Pernia
NextPort, Geneva, Switzerland
e-mail: oscar.pernia@next-port.com

S. E. Larsen
A.P. Moller – Maersk, Copenhagen, Denmark
e-mail: Steen.Erik.Larsen@maersk.com

© The Author(s), under exclusive license to Springer Nature Switzerland AG 2021
M. Lind et al. (eds.), *Maritime Informatics*, Progress in IS,
https://doi.org/10.1007/978-3-030-72785-7_3

1   The Port of Today and Tomorrow as a Multidimensional Hub

Maritime transportation clients expect the system to operate as predictably and reliably as possible. In the end-to-end supply chain, maritime transportation is often combined with other means of transport. Ports, as such, are multidimensional hubs where their core role is to enable the smooth movement of cargo within a supply chain from point of origin to destination. Transhipment is the activity by which cargoes or passengers are moved to another carrier, of the same or different mode. A port is multidimensional in that it relies on the use of information systems for the effective integration of relevant processes to support an efficient "green" supply chain.

The maritime sector is highly self-organised (Watson et al. 2021) and information often exists in siloes. Information exchange can be a challenge within the maritime, logistic, and port environment. Information exchange is mostly based on contractual agreements between parties. This creates the siloes and information 'islands' as the various actors have different contractual partners with very little common ground to exchange information. This legacy is one of the biggest challenges to creating an integrated, holistic approach to port management, with its complex stakeholder landscape, in the overall transport ecosystem. In addition to technical connectivity issues and lack of standardisation there is a need to persuade the whole set of stakeholders to look beyond their contracts to see how their data can contribute to the efficiency of the overall ecosystem.

The concept of maritime informatics makes best use of digital collaboration using data driven decision-making and data analytics. Maritime informatics is an enabler and an evolution linking the myriad of participants together to provide value to sea transport (Lind et al. 2021b). Within ports there are different information technology systems, such as Port Community Systems (PCS),[1] Terminal Operating Systems (TOS), Port Management System, Traffic Control and Management Systems, Single Window Systems, real-time based coordination tools, and automatic systems such as auto-gates. These are examples of effective systems that eliminate siloes and implement the concepts of maritime informatics. As digitalisation in the maritime sector advances, more opportunities for maritime informatics capabilities will emerge.

Currently, much of the debate associated with a port's performance is through the lens of the port as a window to the sea. However, taking a perspective on the port as having a role in the larger cargo chain, the interface towards different means of transport modes needs to be acknowledged. In addition, ports may have many types of cargo throughput, with different terminals supporting the cargo (coal, bulk, passenger, container, and so on). This increases the variation and complexity for each of the actors working within a port. For all port visitors, irrespective of mode

---

[1]https://ipcsa.international/pcs/pcs-general/.

and cargo, enabling episodically tight coupling is a key fundamental goal of maritime informatics.

Further, empowered by maritime informatics, new opportunities arise for the port of not just being a physical transport hub, but also an information hub providing situational awareness on the operations pursued within the port (Lind et al. 2020a). Building on existing systems operating within the port, such as PCS and TOS, and other data may be provided to any of the stakeholders that are in direct interaction (such as shipping companies, truck and railway operators), or indirect interaction (such as beneficial cargo owners), with the port. As data become available from different port assets, Internet of Things (IoT) devices, monitoring equipment and more, there is a requirement to ensure that data can be exchanged among parties that require it in a manner that ensures commercial confidentiality and transparency. In the current situation that is often not the case. Even exchanges among systems from the same manufacturer may be complicated due to different configurations.

Ports are also energy hubs and, as such, can facilitate renewable energy and alternative fuels for associated infrastructure, ships, transport within the port, and all vehicles to and from the port. Presently there is a heavy dependence by maritime shipping on fossil fuels. With the growing demand for cleaner energy, ports are challenged to offer fossil-free energy, such as "green" electricity and hydrogen, in the long run, while facilitating transition fuels like (Bio-) LNG (liquified natural gas) in a shorter timeframe. Channelling demands, improving asset utilisation, optimising storage, and supporting the provision of diverse fuel and power packs needs to be efficiently managed, providing a core role for maritime informatics. The port can be an important enabler for the "green" conversion necessary for a sustainable transport system on a global level. The port as a multidimensional hub also contributes to a number of the 17 Sustainable Development Goals (SDGs) and 169 related targets in the UN Agenda 2030 that is mobilising efforts to end all forms of poverty, fighting inequalities, and tackling climate change.

2 The Port as a Network of Networks

Within a port a multitude of incumbent actors provide services to visiting actors, providing the role of a transport hub. Seen from the transport chain perspective, a transport hub is an intermediary destination, an intermodal hub where the mode of transport is changed. Ports (terminals) may also provide storage and added value for the goods that pass through them. This added value can be through services to the goods or people being transported (such as storage, inspection) or to the asset being used in the transport (such as providing repairs, inspections).

There are many actors that need to collaborate within a port sector, all of whom have their own socio-technical-ecological system (Haraldson et al. 2021), which is typically a key factor in how a port co-produces value for its clients. While the port is an organisational network, constituted of multiple organisations within an ecosystem (network), the port is also part of the larger transport ecosystem (network). As a

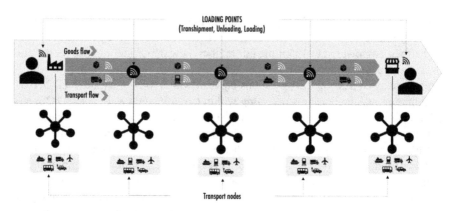

Fig. 1 The port as a transport node in the transport chain

co-producer of value for a part of the value chain, the port constitutes a node in the larger transport chain (Fig. 1).

From a holistic perspective, as well as from a maritime point of view, there is no overarching coordinating body, who acts to ensure that all mechanisms are aligned. This means international logistic partners are less interested in local solutions as they look for solutions (and standards) that can be applied at least regionally (for hinterland partners) or globally (for global carriers). The transport sector is thus a networked organisation, or ecosystem—"... a set of relationships among different organisations that interact with varying degrees of an arm's length relationship typically found in a market" (Watson et al. 2021).

Building upon the networked society (Castells 1996), a port can be conceived as a node in a larger network, and a port is also a network of actors. It is a "flat organisation" of which the different actors have a market-based type of interaction rather than hierarchical power (Williamson 1979). Castells' (1996) argument that new media and communication technologies based around networks are contributing to a fundamental change in culture, maritime informatics provides the foundation for shipping to function as a networked society. Castells' and Williamson's viewpoints should also be considered in the light of the need of new technologies, international policy developments, and data standards. The requirements for many ports are changing.

There is also a differentiation within a port in terms of consideration of its roles and responsibilities. Ports handle regulatory and safety tasks, as well as management of infrastructure as per national, regional, and local legislation. These requirements may differ from port to port to reflect regional or national legislation or local bylaws. The port regulatory responsibilities may include granting safe entry and exit of vessels, persons and goods. Port authorities may also have an operational role with business, which relates to the facilitation of trade or traffic flows. Some ports, as information hubs, connect local communities, as for example the International Port Community Systems Association's (IPCSA) Network of Trusted Networks interconnecting Ports and their customers globally (PortTech 2020).

New technologies are evolving every day, allowing even more data to flow at increasing rates. New technologies are often developed by technical experts for the maritime sector with limited input from maritime subject matter experts. Data may be supplied in proprietary formats, which can limit the efficiency of episodic tight coupling. There is an urgent need for standardised data exchange formats.

The work of the International Maritime Organization (IMO) on e-navigation, including the identification of a series of maritime services (Lind and Renz 2020), has led to the development of internationally agreed standards, including standards specifically designed for the exchange of maritime data in port environments (S-100 series) (Bergmann et al. 2021). Data exchange cannot be considered in isolation from the requirement for processes that support consistent, safe, secure, and effective data exchange among trusted sources. Business initiatives (such as the Protect Group[2]) created harmonised implementation guides for some standards.

It is imperative that both Business-to-Government and Business-to-Business data and information are considered together as much of the data is the same and to truly network the networks in a port these need to be considered together.

3   Ports as Hubs for People, Cargo, Information and Energy Exchange

The different dimensions to the port reflect the many services that the port provides or supports. This includes not only the traditional perspective of the transfer of people and cargo, but also acting as a hub for information collection, analysis, and dissemination as well as energy exchange.

3.1   Ports as Transport Hubs

Ports, or at least the services a port provides, are a resource shared among the many parties that utilise the port as a part of their transport chain working within the various regulatory and legislative requirements governing trade. Ports often depend on infrastructure development policy and investments by governments or external boards, which may provide opportunity for development while also presenting constraints on the use of the infrastructure, expansion or data sharing opportunities.

Ports provide infrastructure and resources ideally to support:

- Safe and secure transit of transport modes, providing a suitable mix of aids to navigation and services to address port user requirements;

---

[2]https://www.protectgroup.co.

- Smooth and timely turnaround processes for visiting carriers independent of mode of transport;
- Efficient and secure handling of cargo or passengers;
- A geographical site where physical services, such as storing and refining, of products may occur;
- Provision of transport-related services like supplies, maintenance, and repair;
- Information services to enable visibility to port clients in terms of cargo or people traceability and administrative cost minimisation;
- Organise pre- and on-transport connections operating in a secure, reliable, and efficient way;
- Streamlining processes with cross-coordination between all actors and organise administrative procedures that are simple and reliable.

Low costs and predictable operations on transhipment services are requirements that have always been present in ports, exist today, and will be valid for ports of tomorrow. All types of carriers expect to be served just-in-time by the port to minimise their idle time, as addressed in concepts for port call optimisation/port collaborative decision making (Lind et al. 2019b). This process supports a carrier network that is cost effective and sustainable. This drives the port to ensure that infrastructure and resources are balanced in relation to the demand and that buffer zones are kept to a minimum. There is now increasing emphasis on the capabilities of digital twinning of ports (Lind et al. 2020b) as a maritime informatics concept that can provide a basis for strategic decision-making on necessary infrastructural investments to meet future demands. Those decisions may concern resource allocation and service trade-offs as an evolution to using simulation for scenario planning assessment, but also for monitoring of port infrastructure, improving operational processes (e.g., detailed real-time weather information), strategic planning and simulation, and function as a basic building block for autonomous transport.

Carriers visit different transport hubs, and if there is any delay in a previous visit the carrier will be delayed to the next transport hub with a flow-on effect to other carriers within each of the transport hubs. Throughout the movement in a transport leg there might be delays due to different circumstances, such as weather conditions, accidents, or limited capacity of natural or physical infrastructures used to move the carrier. This means the originally planned time of arrival may not be reached and the involved actors need to have the capability to share information on the changes to the schedule and to re-plan. This also goes the other way around. Crane malfunction, adverse weather, vessel or equipment malfunctions, peak shortages, etc. also impact port services in such a way that the pre-planned arrival or departure time of vessels needs to be adjusted. It is therefore important that the carrier is informed of deviations as soon as possible so that a vessel's speed can be adjusted to optimise fuel consumption and reduce emissions.

Standardised digital connectivity is critical to support the coordination and synchronisation of physical operations to assure high utilisation of infrastructure and resources. This also includes the management of exceptions and effective introduction of contingency plans to deal with risks that either episodic visiting actors may not show up in time or that infrastructure and resources are not available to provide the agreed services. Each of the actors needs to be informed about what is happening outside their own scope of operations to allow for accurate planning and to enable them to update their plans accordingly. Lately, attention has been given to the synchromodality concept that looks at freight transport as an entire modal network to select the transport modes and routes based on optimisation procedures (Lemmens et al. 2019).

On the agenda for the International Port Community Systems Association (IPSCA) is to provide full transparency in a port environment by informing all the actors of delays, exceptions and other issues relating to the goods being moved. In this context there is also a need to support the regulatory processes that are required for the movement of goods that are outside the control of the supply chain actors, though they have a responsibility for complying with the appropriate processes required in a Port and by national border agencies such as customs. A PCS empowers the collaboration among involved stakeholders to enable the seamless exchange of data to allow for goods to be moved without undue delays. PCS, in combination with maritime informatics, therefore, provides new options to streamline processes with increasing access to real-time data.

A port, similar to many other transport hubs, serves multiple types of trade. Most ports have capabilities to serve container vessels, wet and dry bulk vessel, passenger or cargo ferries, and may even be a cruise ship destination. By being, but not exclusively, a window to sea transport, it becomes essential to assure that the infrastructure for seaside port visits can be handled efficiently. Nowadays we also see that there are substantial investments made to establish intermodal capabilities for managing the transhipment road-to-rail and rail-to-road within the scope of operations for the traditional (sea)port (Fig. 2).

Further, automation is also becoming a must for competitive and sustainable port operations. It may be that there are autonomous carriers, both from the sea and the hinterland side, that put requirements upon the operations pursued at the port in order to be able to pay a visit to the port. We now also see that the handling and storing of goods, as well as in-port transport, is increasingly automated. Again, this requires accurate, reliable, and secure digital data sharing in real time.

Automation relies on effective data and system integration, yet there are many examples where the lack of standardisation on data practices and system interoperability, as well as stakeholder engagement and reluctance of sharing data, (see Sect. 1) create serious constraints for effective port operations and automation. This covers different aspects of automation such as equipment robotisation, process automation, enhanced or automated decision making.

The port as a transhipment hub is a key node providing physical and information services in the larger network of the transport chain. The port itself needs to be coordinated as a network, however, as revealed by Haraldson et al. (2021) and Lind et al. (2021a), ports often do not have a single keystone player. Rather, the provision and coordination of services are distributed among several parties each with varying levels of engagement to other players within a port environment.

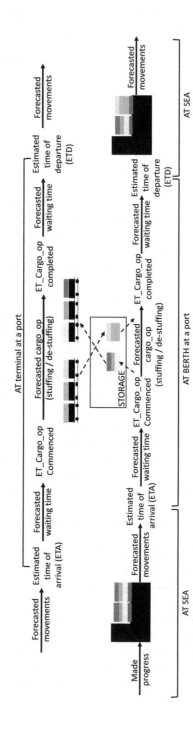

Fig. 2 Movement of containers by ships and trains (as example of carriers) movements with visits to transshipment hubs (ET = Estimated time) (Becha et al. 2020a)

Less developed ports may have less automation, so integration becomes difficult and it may be that they do not have suitable base systems in place such as Port Management Information Systems (PMIS), Terminal Operating Systems (TOS) or similar. Until such systems are in place, these ports will have difficulty competing in the maritime informatics powered shipping ecosystem.

3.2 Ports as Information Hubs

Effective port operation builds on the concept that a port is a network node for providing physical services and should also establish itself as an information hub. Ports as information hubs are key if the desired transparency and predictability along the maritime and transport supply chain is to be obtained.

Efficient port operations are key to the "seamless" transport chain, and digitalisation is the enabler that can realise this potential. As an information hub, working within the scope of its regulatory and governance framework, a port can establish itself as a virtual entity to support high accuracy and efficiency in its operations. This means provision of historical and real-time information associated with, for example:

- Plans and status of the infrastructure (capacity and availability) as well as resources required for serving episodic visiting carriers of different modes of transport;
- Stock-levels for cargo and inventory stored in the port;
- Status of the goods passing through the port and associated processes such as customs paperwork and inspections;
- Plans and status for when particular goods items or passengers are to be served;
- Insight into real time logistic network options for a port regarding seaside connections and hinterland connections;
- Track and trace functionality;
- Insights on plans and movements pursued by the different carriers for different modes of transport making episodic visits to the port;
- Coordination of information for all modes and related services to allow for optimal efficiency and reduced emissions.

A port's efficiency, as well as its ability to innovate, are strengthened through increased digital collaboration and the standardised exchange of data. The digitalisation of the port and its operators enables efficient resource planning, efficient administration in reporting formalities, just-in-time arrivals and departures and operations, traceability in transport, provides support for the port's operations during transhipment, and is an important prerequisite for the port's energy use.

Contemporary emergence of IoT connected devices, including those related to port infrastructure or Smart Containers (Becha et al. 2020a), and supporting technologies, such as 5G, are expected to boost the provision of data. For Smart Containers, there is a need for sensors along the supply chain to pick up data feeds from connected containers. Ports can harvest data from connected containers, when authorised, passing through the port. Importantly, procedures need to be established to determine the authority to share and manage the information that might emerge from a business-to-business interaction. Discussions on data ownership and data sharing are complex, as all parties wish to protect their interests and may fear the opening up of access to data that can be commercially sensitive if combined with other sources.

The digital capabilities of the port are strongly associated to the smart port concept (Lind et al. 2020g). As well, shipping companies and terminal operators are addressing expectations for becoming smarter (Becha et al. 2020b) to ensure integrated capabilities associated to the sea transport. As a result, many parties that see the possibilities for becoming the centre of gravity associated to maritime data. There is a need for neutral parties to facilitate collaboration among the stakeholders of a port, such as port community systems as a local information sharing community.

Supporting humanitarian and global crises has become an issue for ports (Lind et al. 2020c). They are expected to prioritise and fast-track diverse goods intended to alleviate disasters and emergencies. The port therefore also needs to be integrated in horizontal and regulatory based information sharing communities (Lind et al. 2020d; Lind and Renz 2020). By being an efficient producer of information for goods owners, transport buyers, load carrier organisations, etc., the opportunity is provided for information transparency, predictability, and visibility throughout the transport chain, which creates conditions for efficiency and cost minimisation.

As multidimensional hubs, port operations cover many aspects, including the provision of aids to navigation, buoys, lights and Vessel Traffic Services (VTS). These operations make effective use of both traditional systems and, increasingly, digital approaches with automated data exchange from different sensors to provide information that supports a traffic image for the port and its surrounds. VTS acts as an initial contact point for vessels in the port, interacts with many different allied services and supports safe, secure, and pollution free transits.

If ports are to act as information hubs, then key consideration of their digital maturity should be reviewed. A port that is not digitally mature should ensure that core information systems are in place within the port environment and, once those systems and platforms are in place, consider how they can support the operational processes. There are different technology platforms available for use, and opportunities to integrate 'systems of systems' for management of information, monitoring of vessel traffic, and exchange of manifests and other documents.

In order to support global interoperability, information systems should support agreed standards, such as the ones referenced and aligned within the IMO data reference model (c.f. Cauwer et al. 2021) being a part of the mandatory requirements on electronic information exchange between ships and ports that came into effect on 8th of April 2019.[3]

---

[3]https://www.imo.org/en/MediaCentre/PressBriefings/Pages/06-electronic-information-exchange-.aspx.

Introducing digital systems in a connected manner requires a thorough consideration of cyber security, including the protection and authentication of data. This becomes more critical as the ecosystem grows and there is more dependency on the digital infrastructure, increasing the chance that an integrated network may result in passing infractions from one system to other systems. Port and other stakeholders are increasingly aware of cyber security risks and continue to innovate and develop solutions. An example is the Port of Rotterdam FERM initiative (Rotterdam Port Cyber Resilience) which boosts cyber security and resilience in the ecosystem.

3.3   Ports as Energy Hubs

As trade and cargo volumes continue to grow internationally, ports around the globe are looking for new technologies to help manage resources in a more sustainable and cost-effective manner. Maritime informatics is at the core as traditional ports evolve towards being more efficient, effective, technologically advanced and safe. Connectivity and automation achieved through digitalisation helps in reducing the environmental footprint of a port. Sustainable ports are also key to supporting sustainable maritime transport. The different alternative and intelligent innovations in transport systems have a huge potential to reduce pollutants and CO_2 emissions.

An onshore power system (OPS), one such option, can provide a cleaner source of energy to vessels while alongside. However, shipboard power requirements vary from ship to ship. This includes equipment performance parameters and the electricity consumption. Communication between the ship and the shore is key to the successful operation of shore power. Before a vessel arrives at a port, ship and shore need to fully communicate requirements and conduct a compatibility assessment to ensure the safety and success of the shore power supply operation. While alongside, the power requirement of a vessel will vary based on the nature of operations performed. Smart ports are moving from being connected to traditional grids to being part of smart grids. This means that the need for real-time data is ever increasing to facilitate the 'as required' consumption integrated in the system operation. Maritime informatics can provide valuable real-time data required for the synchronisation and optimisation of the use of shore facilities. It can also supplement the interface descriptions, addresses and data type specified under IEC/IEEE 80005-2:2016 for low and high voltage shore connection systems communication where required.

Ports are also the pit stop for carriers, independent of the mode of transport. This provides two opportunities—maintenance and re-fuelling. Offering re-fuelling services is one role for a port for establishing itself as an energy hub. The type of energy it offers would reflect the different types of customers and can include (renewables-produced) electrical power, hydrogen and other types of fossil-free fuel, as well as new "fossil friendly" fuels in shipping such as biofuels and (bio) LNG. These newcomers are less mature and are limited in the current phase. Serving LNG bunkering vessels only exists at dedicated ports, contrary to classical fuel oil suppliers existing in every port. The same applies for facilities such as battery exchange points that currently are in a start-up phase with limited capacities.

A realistic scenario is that a carrier requiring electricity when calling at a port indicates in advance a need for an electrical connection. There are different requirements for electricity, shore power for the ship, power for refrigerated cargo, etc. It would be beneficial if information could be provided to the electricity supplier in advance to avoid the risk of power peaks in the network—which in turn drives up costs and may otherwise affect service continuity. Also, it can be advantageous to supply the carrier with power at an optimal time when the energy demand is low and energy is potentially cheaper, and the financial benefit will be higher for the carrier company. This would accelerate the acceptance and enable the "green" transition for maritime shipping. As an illustration, consider the ferries Tycho Brahe and Aurora which operate on the world's first high-intensity battery-powered ferry line between Helsingborg (Sweden)—Helsingör (Denmark), a voyage that takes 20 min. The ferries have 4.16 MWh lithium-ion batteries on board and a trip consumes about 1.18 MWh. Assuming an energy price of 0.2 Euro per kWh (including taxes), it means a cost of around 400 Euro for a return trip. Since each ferry makes the voyage dozens of times each day, the electricity costs can be millions of Euros per year. Providing electricity to charge ferries when prices are low would be a large saving. Furthermore, the electrical propulsion means, depending on the source of electricity, less pollution and CO_2 emissions.

This simple example gives rise to many follow-up questions related to technology, business models, agreements, planning, distribution, ownership of energy storage, the need for data sharing, and data analytics. Added to this is the possibility for a port to produce electricity, such as by using solar panels, and to store that energy locally using fixed banks of batteries or its idle electrically powered vehicles. Figure 3 is a schematic illustration of the components in a sustainable port seen as an energy hub, where renewable electricity production is in focus. Potentially, solar energy could also be used to produce hydrogen or biofuels that are stored for refilling the ships at appropriate times.

As an energy hub, a port's demand for electricity, as facilitated by the grid as well as other stores of fossil-free energy, will vary over time (Lind et al. 2020e). Electrification of the transport sector increases the need for demand side management, cluster control and energy storage to offer peak load shaving and flexibility. Furthermore, there is a potential to save energy and increase the amount of locally produced renewable energy. Digitalisation is the enabler and opens possibilities to innovative system solutions, intelligent control, and new business models. As there is an exponential development of connected carriers, connected cargo and people, with an increasing number of transactions captured and tracked digitally, the granularity of situational awareness is continually improving. This leads to the possibilities that a port can now develop energy hub capabilities in which energy requirements and distribution are coordinated by digital means, providing information about the timing and volumes of needed energy, and sharing this amongst trusted actors.

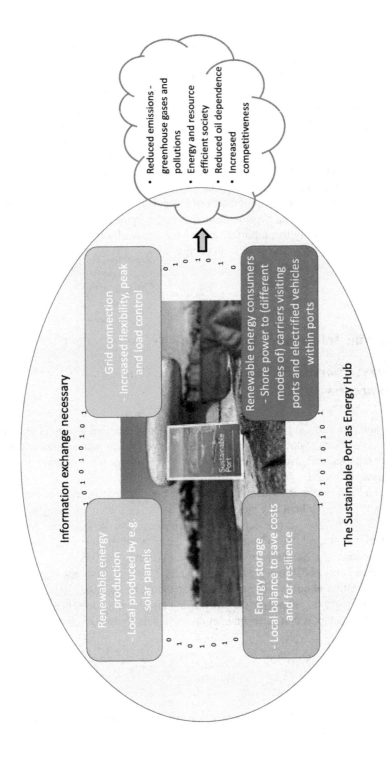

Fig. 3 A renewable energy system for a port (built upon Lind et al. 2020e)

As ports are not energy companies, and electrification most often is not a core competence, there is a need to engage and collaborate with local energy companies. For example, the Hamburg Port Authority has jointly partnered with the local energy supplier to expand the onshore power supply facilities for container and cruise terminals within the port.[4] There is a strong movement to establish collaborative innovation processes between ports and local energy companies. High on the agenda for the energy company is to secure capacity for delivering the electricity needed for a port's operations and its visitors, as well as the placement and ownership of energy storage. The information interface between the different subsystems needs to be defined and standardised and the business models must be worked out. Furthermore, recognising that the energy companies do not only provide electricity to ports, planning must also reflect the requirements of municipal and regional development.

However, and maybe even more importantly, ports, in their capacity as transport hubs, have an opportunity to support a "green" conversion by supplying fossil-free energy to visiting carriers. The port as an energy hub will be an important competitive advantage in the future to meet the requirements of the buyers of transport services.

4 Maritime Informatics Enabling the Networked Port

4.1 The Networked Port as a Provider of Situational Awareness

Ports are one piece in the puzzle to establish situational awareness. Actors in self-organised ecosystems make decisions on their conceived situational awareness. This means that data acquired from operations beyond the scope of what is generated by the organisation is used.

Situational awareness is essential for many of the different operations pursued throughout the supply chain. By situational awareness we mean "knowing what is going on around us", or—more technically—"the perception of the elements in the environment within a volume of time and space, the comprehension of their meaning and the projection of their status in the near future" (Endsley 1995).

As the port is part of the larger transport chain, it is important that it is able to provide information about vessel movements, status and plans associated with the vessels, vehicles, goods and people that are passing through the port. There are many developments to support enhanced interaction within and between all actors within the port ecosystem:

---

[4]https://www.hafen-hamburg.de/en/press/media/video/expansion-of-onshore-power-supply-in-port-of-hamburg%2D%2D-38063.

- PCS as well as TOS forming a network across different ports (PortTech 2020);
- VTS, pilots, pilot vessels, tugs, and other maritime operations within the port;
- Shipping companies and other carrier companies, having more interactions with ports;
- Information exchange with individual organisations, such as ship agents and terminal operators having business in multiple ports;
- Information exchange between cargo owners or transport buyers and ship agents, and the associated Transportation Management Systems (TMS).

As experienced during the Covid-19 pandemic, the continuous, accurate, and timely flow of information is critical to ensure planning and operations during all conditions, providing business continuity through remote data access and sharing. The failure to share information can result in increased queues for vessel and trucks, lost throughput, increased emissions, and poorer air quality.

It does however seem to be reasonable that the port also provides digital services to the external community, as collective knowledge of the port, about the status and accurate plans of the goods, and not just operations pursued on different carriers passing through the port.

4.2 The Networked Port as an Enabler of Collaborative Alignment

Maritime operations, by their nature, must continuously adapt to new situations (Watson et al. 2021). They must address routine activities and exceptions smoothly, with a need to make and revise decisions on when to set aside infrastructure and resources. These decisions should be based on the latest possible information which can be continuously updated to reflect new and changing circumstances (e.g., UNLOCODE changes during the voyage of a vessel, changes of customs practices, and emerging quarantine requirements). Importantly, independent of whether the information is acquired in a direct peer-to-peer interaction or from information based on complementary sources of data, engaged actors will base their decisions on the best data at hand and, as more information becomes available, amend those decisions to reflect changes in circumstances. It is clear that many information systems are not being updated on such things as arrival and departure times for ships or when operations are planned to be conducted. In some cases, the basic problem is that systems are acting in siloes and decisions are scattered across different software modules. There are also examples where global standards are being implemented on an ad hoc basis, without structured change management processes that allow for changes in information technology systems.

There are also examples where the same organisation or supplier decision domains are not connected in an effective or efficient manner (e.g., cargo discharge decking and cargo load selection). In some instances, there is a combination of automatically populated data and manually entered data, or data that is required to be copied from one online system to another. This introduces increased opportunity for error and jeopardises smooth and efficient port calls. Utilising multiple sources of information to cross-check the data upon which each actor is basing their decision is key to assuring timely and secure operations. At the core of self-organising ecosystems as a dynamic competitive environment is the need for mechanisms of adaptation (Watson et al. 2021).

Engagement in information sharing communities (Lind et al. 2020d, f; Lind and Renz 2020) is an example of a collaborative environment that allows a coordinated approach to support dynamic and effective decision making. This is done when actors align with each other's plans and progress. A successful example of this is Port Community Systems. As the number of connected devices grows, such as smart containers, the accessibility to additional and complementary data sources is expected to increase. and the foundations for smart decisions are increasing substantially. Combining these sources with data captured in systems of records (Mangi et al. 2017) and that generated by systems of production, will provide the essential components needed for optimisation and predictability throughout the maritime transport chain as well as the transport chain across several modes of transport. This, however, requires that it is possible to channel the data from systems of production to systems of records, and that harmonised identifiers exist to match the data from various sources.

The situation might concern a just-in-time port arrival and departure or a passage through confined or restricted waterways. The whole need is based upon the desire to coordinate and satisfy the supply of, for example, port call services demanded by multiple clients and authorities particularly when the demand is for the same services at the same time or the same location. If data sharing is inefficient or limited, then situational awareness is compromised.

The big challenge arises when situational awareness needs to be based on data from a large number of actors who may not all have contractual agreements. Those actors that do not have contractual relationships have fewer incentives to share data. This can jeopardise the collaborative processes needed for the better good, such as the optimal coordination of port operations.

Data sharing can support automated data collection and analysis, identifying solutions to support optimal operations. While there may be individual initiatives to collect data, analyse the data and predict specific events, there is an untapped potential in a predictive supply chain to benefit from increased data collection from many sources. Essentially, many actors are continually working on increasing the accuracy of the prediction and, if information is shared, the accuracy of the resulting prediction can be enhanced. Accurate and timely data are fundamental components of prediction and AI, in combination with historical data, can (temporarily) fill a gap when the real time data is not (yet) exchanged. At the moment the data quality from planning processes is often not good enough. There can be gains realised through not only better data exchange, but also better sharing of data analysis methodologies. Once there is confidence on the predictions, decisions can be made in a proactive manner, rather than a reactive manner.

4.3   The Role of the Port in Short Sea Shipping and Ocean Shipping

Measured by distance, about 70% of all sea transport is short-sea shipping (Michaelides et al. 2021). The shipping industry has experienced how a global pandemic has changed the previous configuration of carrier networks, which switched to more connected and flexible configurations to accommodate volume fluctuations as well as the desire to promote local economies. There has been an approach by countries to try to be autonomous in terms of supply for their basic needs. Particularly where the distance between ports is short, there are many times when a delay and departure in a previous port might be later than the estimated time of arrival to the next port. It also follows that the predictability of port operations will be low when there is a lack of real-time updates, situational awareness, and transparency, leading to limited planning horizons (Lind et al. 2019a). This makes port operations difficult to plan and there is a need for two complementary maritime informatics capabilities:

1. Enable the secure and authenticated sharing of data between ports, such as progress in the previous port and capabilities required to serve the ship in the next port, based on a common object of concern; being the ship that is passing between the ports;
2. Real-time based data analytics for effective re-planning of physical capabilities given new conditions

Data sharing environments not only within a port but expanding beyond the single port and port-to-port, are therefore required. Options include the larger ports, being the gateway to regions, considering the feeder and short seaports as an extension of their own port area and offering customers in the satellite ports, in cooperation with the feeder and short seaports, the same information as in the larger ports, thus creating a virtual port complex. This is one example of a value proposition provided through the integrated operation of maritime informatics. Data sharing networks also offer the possibility for insight on operations and fees, so port customers can select their options based on price and such things as CO_2 footprint.

In short sea shipping, smaller terminal and actors usually have less finance to invest in information systems, digitalisation and automation. Nevertheless, such investment is essential to enable a truly digital maritime eco-system for the benefit of big and small players.

4.4   The Emergence of New Business Models for Ports

Taking a viewpoint of the port as a multidimensional transhipment, information, and energy hub means that a port expands beyond traditional value propositions. Building upon Watson (2020) and Haraldson et al. (2021), several additional business values can be identified (Table 1).

Table 1 Different systems level as a foundation for refined value proposition

Systems level	Role	Additional business value
System of production	Enabler for efficient operations	Cost efficient operations, exposure of the provision of additional services, such as fossil-free fuel for the global community
System of records	Enabler for efficient operations with high resource utilisation Provider of supply according to demands (Sub) provider of situational awareness	Sharing of plans and conducted operations Capturing needs of services and provision Enabler of the coordination and synchronisation of infrastructures and resources
System of inquiry	Analytical services filling the gap of missing information for situational awareness	AI-based services combining historical and real-time information for predictions
System of framing	Foundation for framing the port as a transparent and open environment	The repertoire of services framing the port as a multidimensional hub
System of engagement	Open, transparent, and fair data sharing allowing for participation	Overcoming the barriers of data sharing beyond contractual relationships

A port's customers seek opportunities for services that meet their demands. These may include maintenance, energy provision, and other types of carrier or crew specific services. For the port of tomorrow, it is therefore essential to develop a means of matching services to address demand and supply. Here there are two options for the port to consider; to expose its services repertoire directly to visiting clients in, for example, a mobile application, and to expose their services through marketplace applications. One example of the latter application would be Bunkerspot (www.bunkerspot.com) that provides a Bunkerspot Price Index (BPI) capturing daily bunker prices and historical price information across the key fuel grades at 350+ ports around the world. Such a match-making site enables carriers to plan visits to different ports across the world and to seek an optimal price.

Transparency and predictability of operations also enables possibilities for ports to expose their slot capabilities in an open market. Building upon Lind et al. (2021a), a marketplace for trading slot times would satisfy the needs of time slot allocation. "Specifically allocating slots by time and place can enable ports to better coordinate the planning and utilisation of the available resources for all the planned episodes of tight coupling" (Lind et al. 2021a). Such slot times, however, need to be managed dynamically and with flexibility to allow for dynamic planning on a multi stakeholder data platform. Marketplace driven slot times would be an enabler for taking the necessary steps to move from the "first-come, first-served" basis or the rigid slot planning that some ports apply in the container segment, to a logic that builds upon more planned yet flexible port visits. Importantly the slot times need to be based upon a continuous possibility to dynamically replan, where the original slot time is used primarily as a baseline. A slot time marketplace could be established to enable the right to use a slot to be traded to increase decision making flexibility.

5   Concluding Words

We have exposed the opportunities arising from considering the port as a multidimensional hub; a transport hub for the physical services, an information hub for digital services, and an energy hub enabling a "green" conversion. All of these hub competencies require digital capabilities. Key is regarding the port as an integrated part of the transport chain and as having a role in relation to the different stakeholders of the port; including the beneficial cargo owner. Further, as the port is a network, it needs both to assure continuous data sharing between the permanent actors that constitute the port as well as creating network effects by implementing principles of digital collaboration and data sharing to episodic tightly coupled port visitors. This ensures efficiency in physical operations, supports continuous review, and optimisation of strategies and provides new, value adding, services.

As elaborated substantially in the first book on maritime informatics (Lind et al. 2021b), standardisation is key to establishing transparency throughout the maritime supply chain. Common definitions, standards for messaging and interfacing, are also key in ports' development as multidimensional hubs. Importantly, however, is to remember that the end goal is to assure high capital productivity through transparency and predictability in the sustainable movement of goods and people. This should create the incentives for the stakeholders to participate in digital data sharing beyond their contractual relationships and it will likely require amendments to the current ways of working and organising.

Maritime supply chain visibility requires the adoption of maritime informatics principles of digital collaboration, data sharing, and data analytics. Maritime informatics can enable a port to make conscious decisions on how to balance capital productivity and energy efficiency (Lind et al. 2020h), both internally and for their stakeholders, by ensuring capabilities of being a network in the larger network of transport operations.

Ports are an important intermediary in the supply chain. Both as a provider of efficient cargo operations, an enabler for sustainable transport operations, as well as an enabler of the "green" conversion. The port of the future needs to have the capabilities of satisfying the needs of efficiency, sustainability, and resilience empowered by maritime informatics. These new developments need to be safeguarded by an optimal cyber security focus to ensure secure, authenticated and tamperproof data exchange.

References

Becha H, Frazier T, Lind M, Schröder M, Voorspuij J (2020a) Smart containers and situational awareness. Smart Maritime Network, 12 Aug 2020. https://smartmaritimenetwork.com/2020/08/12/the-cargo-owners-case-for-smart-containers/

Becha H, Lind M, Simha A, Bottin F (2020b) Smart ports: on the move to becoming global logistics information exchange hubs. Smart Maritime Network, 20 Apr 2020. https://

smartmaritimenetwork.com/2020/04/20/smart-ports-on-the-move-to-become-global-logistics-information-exchange-hubs/

Bergmann M, Primor O, Chrysostomou A (2021) Digital data sharing for enhanced decision making, chapter 10. In: Lind M, Michaelides M, Ward R, Watson RT (eds) Maritime informatics. Springer, Cham

Castells M (1996) The information age. Economy, society and culture. Vol 1: the rise of the network society. Blackwell, Oxford

Cauwer ND, Fontanet M, Abril J, Greven JT, Juhl JS, Probert S, Renz M, Rødseth ØJ (2021) The IMO reference data model—one solution fits most! In: Lind M, Michaelides M, Ward R, Watson RT (eds) Maritime informatics: additional perspectives and applications. Springer, Heidelberg

Endsley MR (1995) Toward a theory of situation awareness in dynamic systems. Hum Factors 37 (1):32–64

Haraldson S, Lind M, Breitenbach S, Croston JC, Karlsson M, Hirt G (2021) The Port as a set of Socio-Technical Systems: a multi-organisational view. In: Lind M, Michaelides M, Ward R, Watson RT (eds) Maritime informatics. Springer, Heidelberg

Lemmens N, Gijsbrechts J, Boute R (2019) Synchromodality in the Physical Internet—dual sourcing and real-time switching between transport modes. Eur Transp Res Rev 11:19. https://doi.org/10.1186/s12544-019-0357-5

Lind M, Renz M (2020) Do maritime authorities have a role in digitalization of shipping?—the "Digital (port) Approach" in a sea transport context. Smart Maritime Network, 2 July 2020. https://smartmaritimenetwork.com/wp-content/uploads/2020/07/The-digital-approach-in-context.pdf

Lind M, Ward R, Bergmann M, Haraldson S (2019a) How to boost port call operations. Insight no 10, Global Maritime Forum. https://www.globalmaritimeforum.org/news/how-to-boost-port-call-operations

Lind M, Ward R, Bergmann M, Haraldson S, Zerem A (2019b) Digitalizing the port call process, UNCTAD Transport and Trade Facilitation Series No. 13, UNCTAD. https://unctad.org/en/pages/PublicationWebflyer.aspx?publicationid=2663

Lind M, Lehmacher W, Haraldson S, Fu X, Zuesongdham P, Huesmann R, Fich S (2020a) Smart ports as lighthouse nodes of supply chain networks. Port Technology International—The e-journal of ports and terminals, Edition 104-2020. https://www.porttechnology.org/technical-papers/smart-ports-as-lighthouse-nodes-of-supply-chain-networks/

Lind M, Becha H, Watson RT, Kouwenhoven N, Zuesongdham P, Baldauf U (2020b) Digital twins for the maritime sector. Smart Maritime Network, 15 July 2020. https://smartmaritimenetwork.com/wp-content/uploads/2020/07/Digital-twins-for-the-maritime-sector.pdf

Lind M, van Gogh M, Becha H, Kouwenhoven N, Lehmacher W, Lund E, Mulder H, Murphy N, Simha A (2020c) Information sharing communities for digitally enabled supply chain visibility, Article No. 64 [UNCTAD Transport and Trade Facilitation Newsletter N°88—Fourth Quarter 2020]. https://unctad.org/news/information-sharing-communities-digitally-enabled-supply-chain-visibility

Lind M, Becha H, Simha A, Bottin F, Larsen SE (2020d) Digital containerisation. Smart Maritime Network, 18 June 2020. https://smartmaritimenetwork.com/wp-content/uploads/2020/06/Information-transparency-through-standardized-messaging-and-interfacing.pdf

Lind M, Pettersson S, Karlsson J, Steijaert B, Hermansson P, Haraldson S, Axell M, Zerem A (2020e) Sustainable ports as energy hubs. The Maritime Executive, 27 Nov 2020. https://www.maritime-executive.com/editorials/sustainable-ports-as-energy-hubs

Lind M, Becha H, Simha A, Bottin F, Larsen SE (2020f) Smart decision-making and collaborative alignment. Smart Maritime Network, 20 Aug 2020. https://smartmaritimenetwork.com/2020/08/20/smart-decision-making-and-collaborative-alignment/

Lind M, Gardeitchik J, Carson-Jackson J, Haraldson S, Zuesongdham P (2020g) 'Get Smart'—Developing smart maritime ecosystems. Seaways, July 2020. www.nautinst.org/seaways

Lind M, Watson R, Chua CP, Levy D, Theodossiou S, Primor O, Picco A (2020h) A primer for a profitable and sustainable maritime business. Smart Maritime Network, 9 Sept 2020. https://smartmaritimenetwork.com/2020/09/09/prime-considerations-for-shipping-success/

Lind M, Ward R, Watson RT, Haraldson S, Zerem A, Paulsen S (2021a) Decision support for port visits. In: Lind M, Michaelides M, Ward R, Watson RT (eds) Maritime informatics. Springer, Heidelberg

Lind M, Michaelides M, Ward R, Watson RT (eds) (2021b) Maritime informatics. Springer, Heidelberg

Mangi L, Swanton B, Van Der Zijden S (2017) What is Gartner's pace-layered application strategy and why should you use it? Gartner

Michaelides M, Lind M, Green L, Askvik J, Siokouros Z (2021) Decision support in short sea shipping. In: Lind M, Michaelides M, Ward R, Watson RT (eds) Maritime informatics. Springer, Heidelberg

PortTech (2020) IPCSA launches the Network of Trusted Networks. Port Technology International, 1 July 2020. https://www.porttechnology.org/news/ipsca-launches-the-network-of-trusted-networks/

Watson RT (2020) Capital, systems and objects: the foundation and future of organizations. Springer, Cham

Watson RT, Lind M, Delmeire N, Liesa F (2021) Shipping: a self-organising ecosystem. In: Lind M, Michaelides M, Ward R, Watson RT (eds) Maritime informatics. Springer, Heidelberg

Williamson OE (1979) Transaction-cost economics: the governance of contractual relations. J Law Econ 22(2):233–261

The IMO Reference Data Model: One Solution Fits Most!

Nico De Cauwer ⓘ, Martina Fontanet ⓘ, Julian Abril Garcia, Hans Greven ⓘ,
Jeppe S. Juhl ⓘ, Sue Probert ⓘ, Mikael Renz ⓘ, and Ørnulf Jan Rødseth ⓘ

1 Digitalisation of Shipping and the Role of the IMO

The world has more than 8000 ports (Lloyds 2019). Each has different administrative and operational functions and requires various levels of information from and about a ship before it can enter the port. In addition, ships exchange information with each other as well as with other shore functions (Fig. 1).

These information exchanges are increasingly digital. However, many different organisations are responsible for specifying the digital interfaces and most are

N. D. Cauwer
IPCSA, supported by Port of Antwerp, Antwerp, Belgium
e-mail: nico.decauwer@portofantwerp.com

M. Fontanet · J. A. Garcia
International Maritime Organization, London, UK
e-mail: mfontane@imo.org; jabril@imo.org

H. Greven
Netherlands Customs Administration, Apeldoorn, The Netherlands
e-mail: jth.greven@douane.nl

J. S. Juhl (✉)
BIMCO, Copenhagen, Denmark
e-mail: jsj@bimco.org

S. Probert
UN/CEFACT, Geneva, Switzerland
e-mail: suesiprobert@live.com

M. Renz
Swedish Maritime Administration, Norrköping, Sweden
e-mail: mikael.renz@sjofartsverket.se

Ø. J. Rødseth
SINTEF Ocean, Trondheim, Norway
e-mail: OrnulfJan.Rodseth@sintef.no

© The Author(s), under exclusive license to Springer Nature Switzerland AG 2021   61
M. Lind et al. (eds.), *Maritime Informatics*, Progress in IS,
https://doi.org/10.1007/978-3-030-72785-7_4

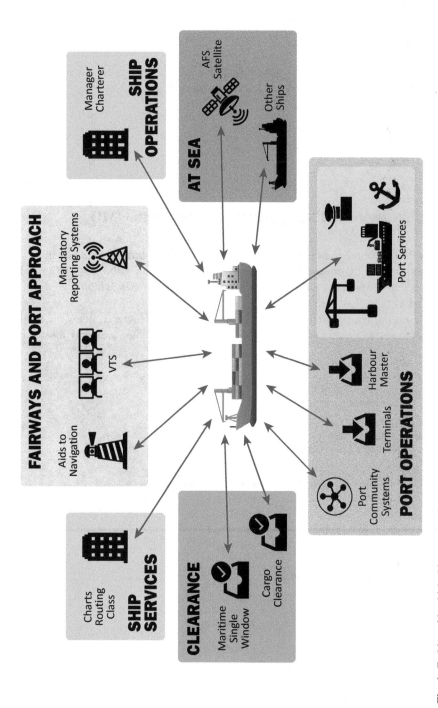

Fig. 1 Entities with which ships communicate

operating on a local or a regional level without involving relevant international standards organisations. If this continues, the lack of standardisation may become a bigger problem than the lack of digitalisation itself!

For internet and smartphone users, the billions of connected units create an ecosystem that supports a natural evolution of standards. This is not likely to happen in shipping, with slightly less than one hundred thousand ships in the world (UNCTAD 2020). There is a very immediate need to focus on international standardisation, and the IMO plays a central role in this. Data exchange standardisation is the second bottom layer of the Maritime Informatics stack (Watson et al. 2020), and without it, upstream layers, such as data mining and decision support, are limited in their scope.

The main purpose of the IMO is to encourage and facilitate the general and international adoption of the highest practicable standards in matters concerning maritime safety, efficiency of navigation and the prevention and control of marine pollution from ships. The IMO is also empowered to facilitate international trade by simplifying administrative and legal matters related to these purposes. These matters all contribute to meeting the UN 2030 Agenda for Sustainable Development and to several of its associated sustainable development goals (SDG).

Ships carry 90% of world trade, including large amounts of food. Thus, shipping is vital to feeding the world (SDG 2). At the same time, the climate action goal (SDG 13) calls for full or almost full elimination of CO_2 emissions, including those from shipping. This requires new fuels and other technologies, but also a massive optimisation of operations to reduce unnecessary energy use. This is not possible without digitalisation and automation to greatly improve the productivity of the most important infrastructure for efficient global trade (SDG 9)—our ports and cargo ships.

In the IMO, digitalisation of shipping and the ship-port interface is developed across several of its committees. The Maritime Safety Committee (MSC) is responsible for safe and efficient navigation and has developed the e-navigation concept to enhance the navigational safety of ships while simultaneously reducing the burden on navigation officers.

The Facilitation Committee (FAL) is responsible for the facilitation of international maritime traffic. This includes international requirements for electronic port clearance. This was included as amendments to the FAL Convention in 2016 (FAL 1967) which required public authorities to establish systems for electronic exchange of information by April 2019. The amendments also encouraged member states of the IMO to implement a 'Single Window' environment as an effective way of delivering digitalised systems (IMO 2019). To support this, IMO also developed a new version of the Compendium on Facilitation and Electronic Business (IMO 2020a, b). A central part of the IMO compendium is the IMO Data Set (IDS) and the IMO Reference Data Model (IRDM).

2 The Emergence of the IMO Reference Data Model

The IMO adopted the Convention on Facilitation of International Maritime Traffic, the FAL Convention, in 1965 (FAL 1967). This provided standard paper-based forms for the necessary ship reporting formalities. In 2001, the IMO FAL Committee approved the IMO Compendium (IMO 2020a, b). This was a description of how the paper-based forms could be digitalised using the UN Electronic Data Interchange For Administration, Commerce and Transport (UN/EDIFACT) data model. This served parts of the shipping community well for many years. However, by 2016 it was clear that a review of the compendium's format was required and that references to other standards, such as those from the World Customs Organization (WCO) and the International Organization for Standardization (ISO), should be included. This developed into the idea of a specification-neutral Reference Data Model.

WCO agreed to implement this 'eCompendium' but recognised that this mission needed a broader approach and involvement from more partners, including fellow standardisation bodies: The United Nations Economic Commission for Europe (UNECE) and ISO, maritime administrations, and trade associations. The core group of domain experts included BIMCO, representing the shipowners, and the International Port Community Systems Association (IPCSA), as well as experts from IMO Member States.

An important challenge was how to deal with the existing standards and the impact on the different standard data models already in use. These data models have been implemented to reflect the specific focus of the various organisations involved in different aspects of maritime activities. For example, the WCO data model represents the requirements of customs organisations and regional authorities, whereas UNECE's UN/CEFACT data model focuses on trade and transport procedures and regulations. It was obvious to all parties that the impact on the existing models must be kept as small as possible.

The key word became 'harmonisation', which has nothing to do with the technology for data exchange, but everything to do with semantics and speaking the same "language". This is what makes harmonisation so vital in developing interoperable technical standards. Technology represents the mechanism by which standards are implemented; as new technologies emerge and new ways of exchanging data evolve, new standards will be needed. Harmonisation, a clear data model structure and clear procedures for maintaining it, are vital for interoperability between different domains and between different technologies (Cauwer and Morton 2019). Thus, the focus of the eCompendium became the IMO Reference Data Model and the corresponding IMO data set.

There are several examples of other subdomain developments similar to the IMO approach. For example, the industry group called SMDG (2021) works mainly on data models for the shipping container sector. Also, the PROTECT Group (2021) works on the standardisation of interactions between private businesses, governments, and port authorities. However, while internationally used standards have been developed and implemented for decades, they always have been used within a specific maritime subdomain. Until now, there has not been an overarching global reference model such as the IMO Compendium that includes all relevant data elements and data definitions.

Having started with the data elements from the FAL Convention and recognising the vital importance of the reference data model, it became clear that the work to harmonise standards should continue. A consensus grew to expand the data model beyond that required by the FAL Convention, thereby supporting standardised and harmonised digitalisation of other areas of ship transport operations. In 2019, the IMO established a special Expert Group on Data Harmonisation (EGDH), under the auspices of the FAL Committee, that was tasked with expanding the range of the IMO Reference Data Model (IRDM).

A topical example that can be highlighted is the harmonisation work being carried out by the EGDH on the Maritime Declaration of Health (MDH). In the light of the enormous impact that COVID-19 has had on international travel, the importance of the EGDH's harmonisation efforts becomes obvious. This work will be the basis for a short-term creation of a global standard for future specific MDH-messaging and worldwide reporting to authorities—a true digital transformation.

Since 2014, the FAL Committee agreed that electronic ship certificates should be treated as equivalent to traditional paper certificates (IMO 2016). All ships are required to carry certificates that establish their seaworthiness, type of ship, competency of its seafarers, and so on. To facilitate the exchange of information related to certificates and access to e-certificates, the data set of a ship's certificates is also included in the IRDM.

Rather than the divergence seen over the past years and the complexity of practical electronic information exchanges resulting from the different data models, WCO and its partners had to find a way to streamline this process to achieve harmonisation and convergence. This was done by building and providing links to all the relevant standards and the data models of the standards organisations. The solution was to establish a new level sitting *above* the 'low level' architecture of these existing data models. And so, the IMO Reference Data Model was born.

The joint approach and co-creation of the model, through the IMO, and in conjunction with a broad group of stakeholders and maritime experts, is a 'first' for the industry.

3   Reference Model Design Principles and Resulting Architecture

The IRDM was originally derived from the FAL Convention (FAL 1967) and the IMO Compendium (IMO 2020a, b) by analysing the data elements listed in the various FAL forms. This list was reduced to one entry for each data element and assigned a number, a name, a definition, and detail of how to represent the data element: for example, as a number, a code or a text string (IMO 2020a, b). This was the basis for the IMO Data Set.

Later, the data elements were coordinated and adjusted to, as far as possible, fit into the international standards that are used to implement the relevant data transmission protocols; particularly, the WCO data model, the UN/CEFACT Core Component Library (CCL) and ISO 28005-2. The updated IMO Data Set was also structured into a common data model—the IMO Reference Data Model. The data model and the data set were finally used to update the standards where necessary. This included providing a cross-reference between each standard's data elements and the corresponding IMO Data Set number. The process is schematically shown in Fig. 2.

This means that the data model was constructed from the bottom up, based on the information requirements in the controlling documents, initially the FAL Convention. The data model represents a synthesis across various organisations' data models as defined by their controlling documents (Fig. 3).

The process resulted in semantic interoperability between the involved standards in this area. This in turn means that reports delivered in ISO 28005-2 or in UN/EDIFACT can easily be mapped to the correct data element in the database of the Maritime Single Window (MSW). Furthermore, the associated data model defined by the IRDM can, if desired, be used as a readily available 'blue-print' for constructing the MSW's database. This is important to ensure that all national MSWs are requesting the same type of data and in the same format.

Work is now under way to extend the IRDM to other reporting requirements and other ship transport operations. This includes mandatory ship reporting systems, waste delivery, port call information, and more.

The eventual scope of the IRDM can be said to be all information elements where a standardised semantic definition and representation helps to facilitate ship

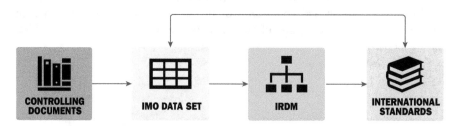

Fig. 2 The data model development process

Fig. 3 IMO Reference Data Model (IRDM) represents the intersection of the standards

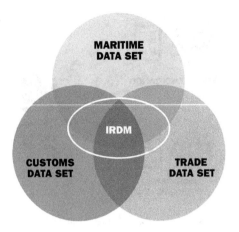

operations and port calls. This means that the IMO committees involved in the maintenance of the model should be broadened to include the Maritime Safety Committee (MSC), in particular its sub-committee on Navigation, Communication, Search and Rescue (NCSR), and the Maritime Environment Protection Committee (MEPC). Correspondingly, additional standards organisations should, when needed, be added to the EGDH.

There are also important benefits in extending the use of the IRDM to some of the e-navigation maritime services. The inclusion of these data sets will link the IRDM to the IHO (International Hydrographic Organization) S-100 framework for e-navigation (IHO 2020) and its Common Maritime Data Structure (Rødseth 2011, 2016).

4 Using the Reference Model: Application Cases

This section describes three use cases for the IRDM, where each is enabled or significantly simplified by the implementation of a harmonised reference model. This shows that the IRDM is a prerequisite for a sustainable and rapid development of a digitalised maritime infrastructure and ecosystem, and also an essential element in the further development of Maritime Informatics Extension, including automation to reduce administrative and operational processes on the ships and in port.

4.1 Harmonised and Interoperable Use of Different Standards

The starting point for the IRDM was to harmonise three international standards for ship to port state reporting (the WCO data model, the UN/CEFACT Core

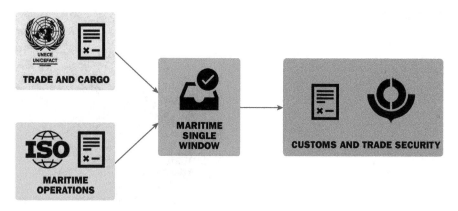

Fig. 4 Interoperability between standards

Component Library (CCL) and ISO 28005-2). A consequence of this is that any of
the standards can be used where it is most suitable without any fear that data needs to
be reported twice or that there are semantic misunderstandings related to some data
items (Fig. 4).

The IRDM has been used as a tool to provide common semantics and representation for the data elements that are needed for the MSW. With mapping tables
provided from each of the organisations between their own codes for the data
elements and the IMO Data Set, achieving full interoperability between the standards
is straightforward.

As the scope of the IRDM increases, such as with the inclusion of electronic ship
certificates and ship-port interfaces, it also becomes apparent that interoperability
between many new actors will become a critical factor in making the shipping
industry more efficient. The IRDM will also facilitate future smarter shipping
operations.

4.2 Reduction of the Administrative Burden

The shipping industry uses significant resources at a substantial cost to comply with
the administrative work imposed by standards and regulations for safety at sea,
maritime security, training, certification and protection of the marine environment.
Port call and pre-arrival reporting are based on national requirements, but shipping is
a global business and truly international solutions are necessary to alleviate the
administrative burdens imposed on seafarers (DMA 2013).

Aboard ship, the preparation of the port and pre-arrival documentation is one of
the most cumbersome administrative tasks. As an example, feedback from ships has
shown that port and pre-arrival documents, even when submitted by e-mail prior to
arrival, do not exempt the ship from submitting the very same documents in hard
copy to the same authority upon arrival. Failure to do so may result in delays, and
sometimes even fines. Seafarers also highlight the differences in formats and forms

used in different countries and ports when, essentially, it is the same data that is required.

A common international solution for a standardised reporting platform, like the IMO maritime single window, would resolve this problem. However, so far most national authorities have developed local procedures and forms and, as a result, there is no consistency or common standard. The development of the IRDM, and the harmonisation of the main standards for electronic ship reporting, has the potential to solve this problem by providing national authorities with an IMO endorsed common data set and associated international standards.

4.3 Just-In-Time Arrival

The basic concept of Just-in-Time Arrival (JIT) is that a ship's the speed is adjusted so that it arrives only when it can proceed directly to a berth or terminal without delay (Watson et al. 2015). This can reduce emissions, congestion in port, and costs.

The JIT concept in the maritime industry is not new. BP Shipping and Maersk tried it out as early as 2009 (MAERSK 2009). While there are obstacles to its implementation (Poulsen and Sampson 2019), today's higher focus on reducing CO_2 emissions makes it interesting to look at speed reductions in the range from 7 to 19% (Jia et al. 2017) (Fig. 5).

To overcome obstacles and provide an effective implementation, clear and frequent communication between all actors in the ship-shore interface before, during and after operations is needed. Actors include ship owners and operators, charterers, ship agents, authorities, port and terminal operators, as well as many ship service providers, such as towage, pilotage, mooring, and more. Harmonised communication between all actors is needed, as any gap in communication may lead to operational inefficiency or even incidents that jeopardise safety or protection of the environment. The ship-port interface is at time of writing being worked into the IRDM and will be standardised by ISO.

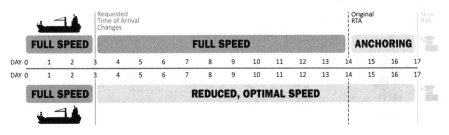

Fig. 5 JIT versus conventional full speed ahead (IMO et al. 2020)

5   Governance and Maintenance

Technology and standards are continuously changing, but those changes will have no impact on the harmonised rules already agreed and recorded in the IRDM.

The advance of technology and messaging brings new and better ways of sharing data, but this also requires the IRDM to ensure the same understanding between new and old parties, whatever new process is integrated into the emerging digital ecosystem for ports and ship operations. The IRDM ensures that when parties do exchange data, they know that the systems are 'talking' about the same things.

It is essential to be sure that these basics are correct and understood in the same way by everybody involved in the domain of maritime informatics. In this regard robust and trustworthy governance and maintenance of the IRDM is of utmost importance (Fig. 6).

5.1   Governance of the IMO Compendium

The IMO Compendium is under the purview of the FAL Committee, which decides on what new data sets are to be included in the IRDM, as well as when they are to be examined by the EGDH, according to urgency.

It was foreseen that the IMO Compendium would cover areas beyond the FAL Convention and the scope of the FAL Committee, and so it is named the IMO, not FAL, Compendium. The electronic exchange of data between ship and shore is required in connection with several other IMO instruments and committees. Accordingly, the FAL Committee at its 43rd session (in 2019) invited other IMO committees and subcommittees to approach it for advice and assistance in preparing the electronic reporting and information exchange requirements for their current and future mandatory instruments. Two examples that are already included in the IRDM are security-related information and the advance notification of waste to be delivered

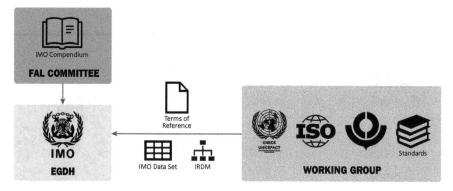

Fig. 6 Main elements in the governance and maintenance of the IMO Compendium

at port facilities. The respective controlling documents are maintained by the IMO under the auspices of its MSC and MEPC.

5.2   Maintenance of the IMO Compendium and Data Model

The IRDM and the IDS are now the main components of the new IMO Compendium. The IMO Compendium must be kept up to date—for instance, when the FAL Convention or any other of the other controlling documents are reviewed and updated. This will often require changes in or updates to the IMO Compendium. Likewise, if errors or omissions in the IMO Compendium are identified, maintenance is needed to correct the data set and model. In addition, when extending the IRDM with new applications, some already existing IMO data elements may need amendment, for example, to be further generalised and reused in the new applications.

Maintenance is needed in all these cases to keep the IMO Compendium up to date. The EGDH is the group which at the IMO level deals with the incremental development of the IRDM. It consists of representatives from IMO member states, the partner standardisation bodies UNECE, ISO and WCO, and of other experts from sister intergovernmental organisations such as the IHO and IALA, and the maritime and port industry, represented through the NGOs (non-governmental organisations) with consultative status at the IMO. The EGDH meets twice a year and its terms of reference are reviewed annually by the FAL Committee. The terms of reference are used to update the scope of the IRDM and to define the relevant controlling documents.

The EGDH follows established working procedures agreed by the FAL Committee which are continuously reviewed as the group gains experience. The EGDH examines and prepares the proposed changes to the IDS and the IRDM and submits them to the FAL Committee for approval.

The modelling of new data sets and its mapping to the main standards takes place after each session of the EGDH. This work is done by the main partner organisations (WCO, ISO and UNECE) and contributing IHO member states and international organisations. From time to time, the partner standards organisations together with interested national or NGO experts meet outside the EGDH meetings to do preparatory work for EGDH.

5.3   Partnership Agreement

In March 2020, to ensure maintenance of the original IRDM as well as alignment with the respective standards, the IMO, WCO, ISO, and UNECE signed a partnership agreement establishing the conditions of cooperation for the maintenance of the IRDM. Through this agreement, WCO, UNECE, and ISO agreed to cooperate to maintain the IRDM and use it as a reference when maintaining their individual standards, in accordance with their respective policies and procedures.

6 Status and Outlook

When the IMO Compendium was designed, a core principle was that it was not to be a 'new' specification but rather a tool to harmonise other technical standards. The goal was to produce a guidance for all interested parties on how to map the data sets arising from the different controlling documents to any of the international standards. This makes it much easier to create software that can communicate no matter what technical standard they are based upon. Hence, any relevant organisation responsible for a standard or a data model in the general scope of the IRDM is welcome to use or contribute to the IMO Compendium.

This open approach can be described as a "bow-tie" concept, having the IRDM in the centre. The data model side is described to the left, whereas the business opportunities leading through implementation is illustrated by the right part of the "bow-tie" (Fig. 7) This also illustrates the potential in developing new opportunities to the right, making use of the data model and corresponding harmonised technical standards to the left.

Common definitions are a prerequisite for harmonisation; the IRDM promotes interoperability; and common definitions and code lists encourage communities to share goals. The larger the scope of the IRDM, the more communities can be accommodated, such as administration agencies, ports, terminal, and other regional or international parties. This obviously also includes the ship owners, managers and charterers. Harmonisation, interoperability, and a large enough community are crucial to an individual organisation's goals of leveraging technology, minimising administrative burdens, promoting digitalisation, and helping all stakeholders meet international standards.

The IMO Compendium is currently covering the information in the seven FAL forms, and expanded information on waste information, health declaration and information on the estimated time of arrival and berth for the JIT concept. During 2020, the EGDH also finalised work on stowaway reporting, the ship certificates that are required to be carried onboard, "acknowledgement receipt(s)" and the "port logistic operational data and real time data".

The IMO's MSC has, through its e-navigation work, approved 16 maritime services based on message exchange between ship and shore. The EGDH has developed or will soon develop data sets for port operational services as well as mandatory ship reporting systems, that can be used to implement some of them. It also approved data sets required to manage automated machine to machine message exchanges. It is expected that these data sets will be approved by the FAL Committee during 2021, but many new data sets are in the pipeline to be adjusted to fit the IRDM.

Looking into the future, we can see more work being done on both e-navigation and other port services that are important for ships. This will make it desirable to

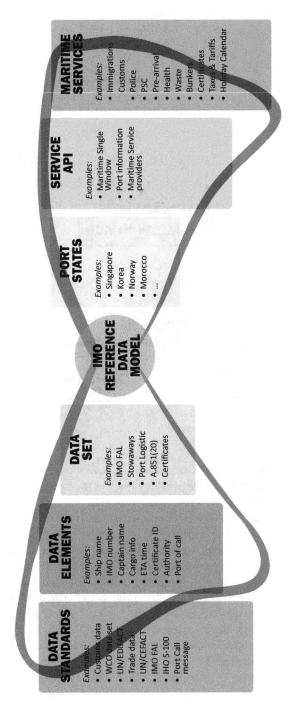

Fig. 7 Illustrating the so-called Bow-Tie Concept, having the IRDM in the centre

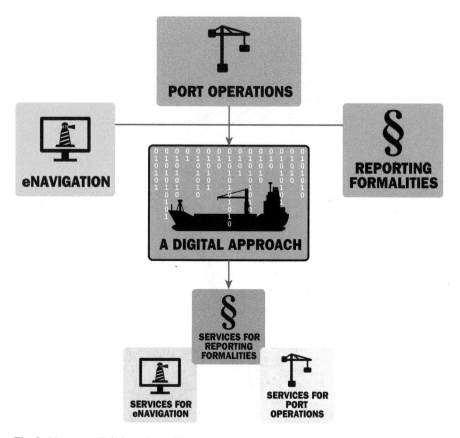

Fig. 8 Many new digital services will emerge

work more closely with the main stakeholder organisations. This includes IMO committees such as the MSC and the MEPC, as well as the International Association of Aids to Navigation and Lighthouse Authorities (IALA), the International Association of Ports and Harbors (IAPH), the International Port Community Systems Association (IPCSA), and many others.

The IHO, which is responsible for coordinating the activities of national hydrographic offices and promoting uniformity in nautical charts and documents through standards, is also defining some operational data in its S-100 framework for maritime geographic information systems (IHO 2020). A link between the IMO Compendium and the product specifications created under the S-100 standards framework will be necessary. Together with developments in the VHD Data Exchange System (VDES), this will give ships another way to exchange relevant digital information with shore-based systems (Fig. 8).

The IMO Compendium is growing. It is the only instrument where different maritime standards organisations can cooperate to develop a common information model with unified semantics that can be mapped to their own respective standards. This can be used not only to translate between the different standards but also as a tool to ensure the same vocabulary when describing data flows, making it possible to integrate the reporting formalities of the authorities with the concepts of e-navigation and the operational needs in the port, enabling a connected and integrated world.

7 Concluding Remarks

Digitalisation is a prerequisite for our modern world, including all parts of shipping. Recently, the COVID-19 pandemic has led to increased focus on the role of digitalisation in empowering maritime operations to become a part of the wider supply chain. Both require smart communication between ship and shore.

There are many examples of data-driven demands faced by the maritime industry today. To name a few, port authorities are using real-time data from across the transportation ecosystem to improve capacity utilisation, energy efficiency, and throughput. Customers are increasingly expecting real-time updates on freight location and delivery dates. Environmental and safety concerns create new reporting requirements. With the extended use of digital data over many domains, it becomes clear that a single technical standard cannot provide the necessary coverage to support all these functions and gain the full benefits of digitalisation.

New systems and applications using onboard sensors can provide more economical operations as well as supporting better predictive maintenance. For the ship operator, this leads to much better usage and management of assets, reductions in unplanned downtime. and a decreased carbon footprint. This has positive safety, efficiency, and environmental benefits that helps to meet society's expectations in relation to the sustainability of ship transport. Looking ahead, smart and autonomous ship trials are proceeding around the world, bringing even more possibilities and challenges for ship operators and others in the sector.

Hence, the maritime industry needs to strive towards solutions that enables smart and seamless exchange of data between all involved parties. International standards are already in use—but these standards are not harmonised between the different standards organisations and the domains they represent. Some of these standards are also adapted only at a local or national level. It is commonly acknowledged that improving the quality and availability of many different real-time operational data is critical to facilitating the arrival, stay and departure of ships, people and cargo. Hence, harmonisation of existing industry standards is required to improve the digital data exchanges.

The harmonisation work—which in fact is 'standardisation of the semantics', as opposed to standardisation of electronic messages—is needed to give the maritime world a sufficiently strong foundation for the implementation of efficient and pervasive electronic business processes.

The work done in IMO on this matter, by the FAL Committee and the EGDH, on the maintenance and expansion of the IMO Compendium, will be instrumental, as

IMO is a UN Agency well respected by its member states and the shipping industry. A central part of the IMO Compendium is the IMO Data Set and the IMO Reference Data Model. The IMO Compendium, and in particular, the IRDM is a central element in this harmonisation. It is a unique and very promising new development in the domain of Maritime Informatics. Digitalisation is happening now: the IMO Reference Data Model is a one-off opportunity for future digital business!

Acknowledgements Part of the work reported on in this text was performed in the AEGIS project, which has received funding from the European Union's Horizon 2020 research and innovation programme under Grant Agreement 859992.

Disclaimer This disclaimer informs readers that the views, thoughts, and opinions expressed in the text belong solely to the authors, and not necessarily to the authors' employer, organization, committee, or other group or individual.

References

Cauwer ND, Morton R (2019) Why standards matter, edn 85. Port Technology
DMA (2013) Danish Maritime Authority. Survey on administrative burdens among international seafarers. Final report—international seafarers
FAL (1967) The convention on facilitation of international maritime traffic (FAL), entry into force 1967, as amended in 2016
IHO (2020) S-100 universal hydrographic data model—what is the IHO S-100 standard? https://iho.int/en/s-100-universal-hydrographic-data-model. Accessed Dec 2020
IMO (2001) The IMO compendium on facilitation and electronic business. Annex to FAL.5/Circ.15, Electronic Data Interchange (EDI) for the Clearance of Ships
IMO (2016) Guidelines for the use of electronic certificates, FAL.5/Circ.39/Rev.2
IMO (2019) Circular FAL. 5/Circ.42 'IMO guidelines for setting up a maritime single window'
IMO (2020a) The IMO compendium on facilitation and electronic business [online]. https://www.imo.org/en/OurWork/Facilitation/Pages/IMOCompendium.aspx. Accessed Dec 2020
IMO (2020b) The IMO reference data model data set [online]. https://svn.gefeg.com/svn/IMO-Compendium/Current/index.htm. Accessed Dec 2020
IMO et al (2020) Just-in-time arrival guide—barriers and potential solutions. IMO
Jia H, Adland R, Prakash V, Smith T (2017) Energy efficiency with the application of Virtual Arrival policy. Transp Res Part D Transp Environ 54:50–60
Lloyd (2019) Lloyd's maritime atlas of world ports and shipping places 2020–2021. Routledge, London. isbn:9780367427108
Maersk (2009) Sustainability report 2009. A.P. Moller-Maersk, Copenhagen
Poulsen RT, Sampson H (2019) 'Swinging on the anchor': the difficulties in achieving greenhouse gas abatement in shipping via virtual arrival. Transp Res Part D Transp Environ 73:230–244
PROTECT Group (2021) http://www.protect-group.org/.
Rødseth ØJ (2011) A maritime ITS architecture for e-navigation and e-maritime: Supporting environment friendly ship transport. In 2011 14th International IEEE Conference on Intelligent Transportation Systems (ITSC), IEEE, 5 Oct 2011, pp 1156–1161
Rødseth ØJ (2016) Integrating IEC and ISO information models into the S-100 Common Maritime Data Structure, E-navigation Underway International 2016; Copenhagen

SMDG (2021) Electronic version. http://www.smdg.org/

UNCTAD (2020) Handbook of statistics. United Nations, Geneva. isbn:978-92-1-112997-7

Watson RT, Holm H, Lind M (2015) Green steaming: a methodology for estimating carbon emissions avoided. Paper presented at the International Conference on Information Systems, Fort Worth, TX

Watson RT, Lind M, Delmeire N, Lieaa F (2020) Shipping: a self-organizing ecosystem. In: Lind M, Michaelides MP, Ward R, Watson RT (eds) Maritime informatics. Springer, Cham

The Role of Industry-Based Standards Organisations in Digital Transformation

Henning Schleyerbach ⓘ **and Henk Mulder** ⓘ

1 Introduction

A digital transformation of the container shipping industry is needed to raise the levels of transparency and thereby improve reliability, efficiency, and customer experience. This, in turn, will fuel the growth and the relevance of maritime informatics as a tool to further continue the pursuit of a reliable, efficient, resilient, ecologically sustainable, and cost-effective industry.

To facilitate and support such a digital transformation and by becoming a collective voice, the largest container lines have founded a non-profit standards body—the Digital Container Shipping Association (DCSA).

The DCSA can be compared with the International Air Transport Association (IATA), which has been instrumental in digitally transforming the airline industry.

This chapter examines the approach of the DCSA and compares it with similar activities in IATA, which has been instrumental in digitally transforming the airline industry—albeit over a longer period of time.

Industry-based organisations, such as the DCSA and IATA, complement inter-governmental organisations, such as the International Maritime Organization (IMO) and the UN Centre for Trade Facilitation and Electronic Business (UN/CEFACT), that are focused primarily upon business to government (B2G) interactions, by monitoring and contributing to standards necessary for business to business (B2B) interactions. Such membership driven organisations are important as the intergovernmental organisations do not normally address specific and detailed

H. Schleyerbach (✉)
Digital Container Shipping Association (DCSA), Amsterdam, Netherlands
e-mail: henning.schleyerbach@dcsa.org

H. Mulder
International Air Transport Association (IATA), Geneva, Switzerland
e-mail: mulderh@iata.org

© The Author(s), under exclusive license to Springer Nature Switzerland AG 2021
M. Lind et al. (eds.), *Maritime Informatics*, Progress in IS,
https://doi.org/10.1007/978-3-030-72785-7_5

implementations in the relevant industrial segments—leaving that area to the industry, which itself knows about best.

The DCSA, similar to IATA, acknowledges the close relationship between software and standards and provides reference implementations and toolkits. To promote the introduction of standards, the DCSA provides open-source software thereby lowering the threshold for everyone to adopt their standards.

The collaboration being facilitated by DCSA, both between shipping lines, as well as with shippers, forwarders, ports, and solution providers, is expected to enhance the quality of the service of container sea transport as part of the multi-modal transport chain.

2 The Need for Digitalisation

The container shipping industry is extremely fragmented in terms of data, processes, and technology. As a result, quality data (or any data at all) regarding the expected arrival at the destination and the current position of a container shipment are often unavailable. Multi-modal transport chains often appear as "black boxes", and shipping containers are lost from view until they arrive at certain points in the supply chain. The reliability of global supply chains is impacted by this lack of transparency, which in turn has a negative effect on business performance for multiple stakeholders.

According to the International Chamber of Shipping (ICS), 90% by volume of world trade is carried by ships (ICS 2014). With the average global schedule reliability of container shipping for some trades as low as 50% (Sea-Intelligence 2019), delays have a negative economic impact not only on individual shippers, but on global economic productivity.

End-to-end container data visibility and transparency would increase shipping reliability, and promote greater efficiency, collaboration and innovation, and greatly improve the customer experience. In addition, it would mitigate some of the adverse impacts that shipping currently has on the environment. This level of transparency, however, requires the exchange of data that is neither available nor accessible to most stakeholders in a shipping transaction. Enabling the efficient, secure, and timely exchange of accurate data between every stakeholder along the end-to-end journey requires a digital transformation of the container shipping industry.

Numerous industries such as banking, telecommunications, and the airlines have benefitted from successful efforts to digitally transform their operations. As with these industries, transforming container shipping requires a global technology framework that facilitates the seamless exchange of data. This framework must have a unified and standardised approach to data communication across all technology platforms, modes of transportation and stakeholders—from carriers and shippers, to ports and terminals, even governments and regulators (Watson et al. 2021).

Recognising this need, 9 of the top 10 global container shipping carriers founded the neutral, non-profit standards body, the DCSA.[1] DCSA's mission is to shape the digital future of container shipping by being the industry's collective voice, working towards alignment and standardisation. By setting frameworks for effective, universally adoptable solutions and innovating, it seeks to enable transparent, reliable, easy to use, secure and environmentally friendly container transportation services. DCSA's open-source standards, free for everyone to use, are developed based on input from DCSA member carriers, industry stakeholders, and technology experts from other industries. These standards ensure the interoperability of technology solutions, and hence, the seamless flow and availability of data.

Since its founding, DCSA has made great strides in creating digital standards for some of the most urgent and impactful aspects of the container shipping industry; however, much still needs to be accomplished. As an example of what is possible in terms of transformation, we can look to a comparable industry: airfreight. Like the role envisaged by the DCSA, IATA has been instrumental in digitally transforming the airline industry.

IATA has a long history of standardisation of industry best practices, including standards for the exchange of electronic information and digitalisation. The IATA Cargo Interchange Message Procedures (Cargo-IMP) for electronic document formats, based on the UN Electronic Data Interchange for Administration, Commerce and Transport (UN/ EDIFACT), goes back as far as the 1980s and are still used for the bulk of data exchange. In the 2000s IATA upgraded these to use eXtensible Mark-up Language (XML), and since 2017, IATA has developed Application Programming Interfaces (API) based data sharing standards called 'ONE Record' (IATA 2021). As a result, all airfreight stakeholders, without exception, accept IATA's standards and leadership in the area of data exchange, and support its developments.

3   Industry-Based Contribution to Standards

The sixth layer of the Maritime Informatics stack (Watson et al. 2021) is data exchange (Table 1). The unstated message of this layer is that data exchange needs to be standardised. Without a common language and format for communicating among parties, the higher layers of data stream mining and decision support cannot function. Such standards need to be global and strongly supported by industry. Consequently, they are the subject of the first layer of the stack. Industry and regulators need to act collectively and globally to create an effective operational data exchange layer that uses international communication networks and their

---

[1]DCSA member carriers include: MSC, Maersk, CMA-CGM, Hapag-Lloyd, ONE, Evergreen, Yang Ming, HMM and ZIM.

Table 1 Layers of the Maritime Informatics stack

	Layer	Design questions
1	Global	Industry-wide international standards for digital data exchange within the maritime sector
2	Regional/National	Design and implementation of policies to support a digitally enhanced maritime sector and a regional/national excellence in Maritime Informatics
3	Structural	Design of structures, such as markets, organisations and partnerships to implement efficiently frequently occurring maritime decisions in a digital era. These include shipping conferences and long-term contracts between shipping companies and terminal operators
4	Decision support	Design of decision processes and associated actions to implement frequently occurring maritime industry decisions
5	Data stream mining	Design of techniques for dynamic identification of model parameters to support real-time decision processes in the maritime sector
6	Data exchange	Design of message formats and content for data exchange between elements of a maritime system to support decision making
7	Data communications	Design of data communication networks to capture data for decision making at the appropriate level of granularity and frequency and transmit control commands to connected maritime equipment and devices

Watson et al. (2021)

associated standards to glue together the many components of the world's maritime industry.

With the aim of creating data exchange standards to facilitate global trade, a number of intergovernmental authorities, standards bodies, and legislators have passed legislation or established standards for different aspects of cargo transportation (for example, the International Maritime Organization (IMO) (Cauwer et al. 2021) and UN/CEFACT). Standards emanating from these inter-governmental organisations normally reflect a larger purview than that of industry-based bodies such as the DCSA and IATA. In general, their efforts are designed to meet the common needs of B2G communication, multiple modes of transportation and can be enforced legally, which has clear advantages. Meanwhile, the industry-based organisations, such as the DCSA and IATA concentrate their efforts on B2B communications and efficiencies. Like airfreight, the container shipping industry has unique requirements for what needs to be digitally transformed (and how), that may not be addressed by the existing overarching regulations.

Industry-based initiatives can support the standardisation process by introducing domain specific knowledge, full-time resources, and a coalition of the willing to adopt and implement the standards. They can focus on the B2B component to improve the customer experience. There needs to be a commitment to continuously maintain and extend standards to cover future requirements. Building standards based on public sector models and incorporating additions in them assures easy and wide adoption. Domain specific additions should focus on customer requirements, with fast and wide adoption as the core value proposition.

Developing global industry standards is as hard as capturing a global market through a product or service. Developing specifications for digital standards requires the input and support from stakeholders across the industry, and for an industry to accept these as leading or even unique standards requires their full trust and commitment.

IATA has built its reputation over three quarters of a century, and its neutrality has been a key ingredient to its ability to develop acccepted standards in the airline industry. The fact that it is industry-based is an important factor: it ensures that the community of stakeholders is limited to its members, and provided that they do not infringe antitrust laws in the process of standardisation, they are not unduly influenced by the much wider and sometimes less committed stakeholders as is sometimes the case with intergovernmental organisations, where every stakeholder group or even citizen may be entitled to express their view and seek to exert influence. Intergovernmental organisations often have significant political hurdles to overcome as well, that may then lead to less-than-optimal compromises.

Industry-based organisations, like IATA and the DCSA, are technically only accountable to their membership, which allows them to focus their efforts on the development of standards that they feel they require. In practice, these organisations still acknowledge the stakeholders far beyond their membership, including in the public sphere, but they do so as needed. This gives them full control over the stakeholder input process.

Another example of the flexibility that industry-based organisations enjoy is the ability for them to cooperate on specific programs for mutual benefit. Any such cooperation can be supported by agreements whose terms are freely determined.

The funding of standards development programmes can also come from various sources, and the private nature of the organisations involved provides for channels that are often not available to public entities, such as funding from revenues from commercial products and services, and partnerships with individual companies.

Lastly, the more significant and well-established members of the industry-based standards organisations that actively participate in the development, testing, and deployment of new standards, bring significant weight to those standards through their endorsement and usage. It is often the critical mass of the combination of these companies that provides the required momentum to ensure the success of any new or enhanced standard.

4 DCSA and IATA: Different Industries, Similar Purpose

Both air and maritime transport are global since the freight and the passengers carried cross borders, continents, and regulatory boundaries. Like IATA, the DCSA envisions its industry as a fully digitally interconnected ecosystem. IATA's 75-year history exemplifies the challenges and the opportunities presented along the path towards achieving such a vision.

IATA's roots lie in the earliest organisation of air transport in the 1920s when aircraft were first being used for passenger transport, airmail, and the transport of goods. Since most transport required more than a single air operator, the early IATA agreed on common standards for 'interlining'—the concept of joint transportation. This included common transport document formats, service standards, and the financial processes for settlement between airlines and their agents.

The jet age introduced the challenge of rapid global transport with the need for information exchange that matched that speed. This coincided with the evolution of digital computers. IATA reacted by coordinating and disseminating digital standards for passenger, freight, and mail transport. Unsurprisingly, this revolutionary move at the time has now created a technology legacy which has become an ongoing challenge: replacing old electronic standards like Cargo-IMP that hail from the telex era to modern data sharing standards, like ONE Record. This is something to try and guard against wherever possible in future standards. Past technology legacies are a significant burden on change management and upgrade costs.

Global air transport is governed by the UN International Civil Aviation Organization (ICAO), which among others things fosters the planning and development of international air transport to ensure safe and orderly growth. It does this by adopting standards and recommended practices concerning air navigation, its infrastructure, flight inspection, prevention of unlawful interference, and facilitation of border-crossing procedures for international civil aviation.

The balancing act between providing common business standards accross a wide group of companies and cooperation with regulators has been central to the longevity and success of IATA. For example, both the liability of carriage of passengers and freight (ICAO business) and the transport conditons and format of air tickets and waybills (IATA business) are important issues to be addressed if air transport is to be successful.

The success of IATA in coordinating, facilitating and implementing standards among its air transport members is at least as much due to its cooperation with regulatory authorities as it is with standards development itself. The ability of airlines to speak with one voice through IATA facilitates regulatory developments. Equally, IATA is able to inform its members of changes in legislation that require their regulatory compliance.

As an example, IATA contributed its experience to the ICAO Montreal Additional Protocol No. 4 (MP4) to the Montreal Convention 1999 (MC99) that limits the liabilities of a carrier and permits the use of electronic air waybills. IATA, through its Cargo Services Conference (CSC) Resolution 600b then adopted the Conditions of Contract for air waybills—thereby encouraging its members towards proper implementation and compliance. The electronic air waybill was also supported by IATA CSC Resolution 672, which provides a Multilateral Air Waybill Agreement that is signed by all freight forwarders and IATA on behalf of its members. This is the contractual document that supports electronic messaging.

The key parallels between air and maritime transport are obvious, but the shared connection between them may be less clear. What brings air and maritime carriers together is that they share the same customer: the freight forwarder. Acting on behalf of shippers, these forwarders require access to all modes of transport and one of their challenges is that the various transport modes curreently operate under different regulatory frameworks, and use different documents, digital standards, and processes.

Although forwarders are expected and are willing to handle such incompatibilities, it is in the interest of all stakeholders to move towards using tools and standards that best support the planning and execution of transport across different transport modes. As global trade becomes increasingly agile due to globalisation, increased e-commerce, advanced digital technologies, and as we have recently experienced due to disruption, such as the COVID19 pandemic, the need for rapid adaptation and flexibility within the transport supply chains is an urgent requirement, if we want to retain a network of independent transport and logistics operators. The alternative could well be a consolidated network that would be less competitive and likely more costly.

For the freight forwarders to innovate their digital capabilities if would be best if they can rely on standards that are common across the transport modes. Standards driven innovation and the aforementioned flexibility will then translate into benefits for shippers and for carriers.

e-Commerce deserves a special mention. In 2019, an estimated 10% of air freight volume was e-commerce and that number is expected to double by 2024. Currently, the big e-commerce providers rely on the global logistics and transport infrastructure for their freight needs. Consumer demand is pushing these e-commerce providers to ever more demanding service quality, and this creates an opportunity and a necessity for the established transport and logistics providers to deliver or to risk seeing business go elsewhere. The indications are that e-commerce providers are not primarily interested in running their own logistics and transport, but it is also clear that they will step in if this is the only way for them to meet their customers' expectations.

The pace of change in the digitalisation of transport has typically been slow. The development of the electronic air waybill described earlier and its industry usage was measured in decades. The program was started before 2000 and is only expected to see 100% penetration by 2022. On the other hand, the annual double-digit growth of e-commerce (which is founded on digital platforms), the rapid assimilation of technology by younger generations and the new imperatives of the need for touch-free cargo due to such things as COVID19, is indicating an accelerating timescale. Can anyone say with certainty that we will still be able to trade and transport with paper-based processes in a decade? Our personal online and digital behaviour leads us to question that outlook. If a decade is too much, what is the likely point of digital transformation of freight and logistics? Our planning should probably aim to half that time.

5 How DCSA Drives Standardisation and the Adoption of Standards

Development of DCSA standards is an agile, iterative, and collaborative process carried out by DCSA in close conjunction with key stakeholders and subject matter experts from member carriers, who need to share their non-commercially sensitive processes and data requirements during the development phase. Common and conflicting data and processes across carriers are identified and mapped, and baseline standards built. These are then validated, aligned and agreed upon by all carriers. Industry feedback is solicited on the initial release and the standards iterated as necessary.

To reach alignment regarding data definitions and data exchange methods across the industry, the DCSA has developed a shared data language and logical data model for container shipping, called the DCSA Information Model (DCSA 2021a). This serves as the foundational data language for the industry. The Information Model is based on the business terms defined in the DCSA Industry Blueprint (DCSA 2021b) and has been mapped by the DCSA against the UN/CEFACT Buy-Ship-Pay Reference Data Model (BSP-RDM) (UNECE 2021) to ensure existing investments are preserved while streamlining communication among all supply chain participants. This mapping is key because it ensures that the same business and data language is spoken across standards.

DCSA data and process definitions can be used separately to standardise and align paper-based processes, with no digitalisation required to gain some measure of efficiency. However, to achieve digital transformation, standards are needed to connect the systems of multiple transport parties. The question then becomes, what is the best approach for standardising the digital exchange of data?

6 EDI Is Now Out of Date

In container shipping, using an electronic data interface (EDI)—the intercompany communication of business documents in a standard format, has been the dominant method for exchanging digital messages between container shipping stakeholders for decades. It was designed to eliminate much of the human error that occurs with manual, paper-based processes, and it does so quite effectively. But, like many 40-year-old technologies, EDI has some drawbacks in terms of keeping up with modern customer demands for visibility and responsiveness.

The limitations of EDI stem from the fact that it was designed for one-way communication of one type of message from one machine to another. Each EDI connection must be integrated into the back-end systems of the sending and receiving parties. A cargo owner needs multiple EDI connections with each carrier with which they work to communicate all the messages involved in, for example, a booking request. And if any of the data in any of the messages changes on either end, or a new type of data is needed, the EDI connection has to be reconfigured, or a new one has to be created.

As a result, the maintenance of EDI is extremely labour-intensive and expensive due to the number of one-to-one EDI connections required to connect multiple parties. Even if companies have the money to spend, it is increasingly difficult to find people who can do the job. Technology is moving forward, and information systems professionals are trained on modern technologies. EDI is a dead end for companies that need to innovate while maintaining a motivated workforce.

7 APIs: Real-Time Interactions, Lower Costs

The Application Programming Interface (API) is the modern standard for interoperable digital communications. It is a set of programming instructions and data exchange standards that allow different connected systems to communicate with each other in real time. APIs can handle billions of interactions every day. With new technologies like smart container tracking devices (Becha et al. 2021), real-time data exchange volumes will grow exponentially, necessitating a shift to API technology.

The value of API technology is well recognised in business, and it has been a linchpin for digital transformation in many digitally advanced industries, such as banking and e-commerce. Think about using a credit card to purchase something online. The data needed to complete the transaction is exchanged and validated instantly over the Internet using APIs. Many standards organisations are embracing APIs as a way of improving information sharing and interoperability. UN/CEFACT has launched efforts to encourage the proliferation of APIs to support international trade and transport processes.

The two-way, real-time data exchange enabled by APIs is needed to increase visibility in container shipping processes and events. Think about the benefits for exception handling. With EDI, shippers must wait for carriers to notify them about agreed-upon events. However, with APIs, shippers can query the carrier's system or subscribe to automatically receive status updates for any relevant event. If there are delays or other types of exceptions, shippers can learn about them as they happen and work to resolve them immediately.

Not surprisingly, DCSA has chosen the API as the preferred method of data communication for its standards. All DCSA digital standards are released with interface standards that include freely available API definitions to facilitate implementation and compliance. API definitions are available to download on the SwaggerHub (DCSA 2021c) open development platform. DCSA also publishes API reference implementations on GitHub (DCSA 2021d) which can be freely downloaded for immediate use and fine-tuned or adjusted as needed.

8   Developing Standards and Software Goes Hand-in-Hand

A central belief of the DCSA is that it is only possible to define technical standards in combination with a reference implementation and a set of tools to validate compliance. This is a long-established principle that can also be found in other technology standardisation organisations, such as the Java Community Process (JCP 2021).

The DCSA has funded the development of a toolkit and reference implementation software. These components are licensed under the Apache License 2.0 so that other parties can freely use, modify, and extend them (Apache 2021)—also for commercial purposes.

The reference implementation serves three purposes:

- it facilitates definition of the standard itself during development;
- it provides a definitive example (for example as an API provider) for software engineers working on integration;
- it allows adopters to compare the behaviour of their implementations with the standard; and ambiguities in the written standard (which are inevitable) can be resolved by observing the behaviour of the reference implementation.

The validation toolkit serves three purposes:

- it facilitates definition of the standard itself. In particular for APIs, it acts as a receiver for notifications, something that is difficult to simulate using standard API development tools such as the Postman API Client (Postman 2021);
- it provides a definitive example of a standards consumer for software engineers developing compliant applications. If their components can pass the toolkit validation tests, then they can, by definition, be considered compliant; and
- it allows standards consumers to compare the behaviour of their implementations with the standards. Ambiguities in the written standard (which are inevitable) can be resolved by observing the behaviour of the validation toolkit.

The components can be integrated to form a working demonstration system, as shown in the following diagram for the case of APIs (Fig. 1).

9   IATA's Development of the ONE Record Data Sharing Standard

IATA started the development of a data sharing standard, ONE Record, in 2017. It focused its technical work on the development of an airfreight ontology (semantic model), an API, and a framework for secure data exchange between airfreight stakeholders.

Unquestionably, the hardest part was developing an understanding of the concept of data sharing in a community of airfreight business and information systems professionals who had worked their entire careers in a data exchange environment

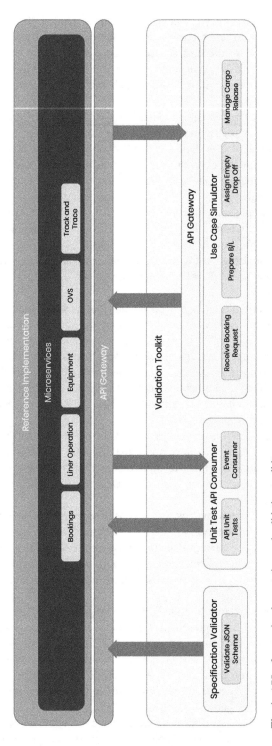

Fig. 1 API reference implementation and validation toolkit

based on EDI messaging. They had no issue with understanding the need for change, but the idea that you do not need to actively push data along a supply chain but instead provide access to the data as needed through APIs has not been an easy transition. In fact, it can be compared to those familiar and comfortable with the 1980s email concept versus those using today's self-service and self-paced social networking platforms.

The development of the semantic models in the airfreight ontology was facilitated by the deep business expertise in airfreight data models on the part of the business and systems stakeholders. One challenge that had to be overcome was that traditional models were based on legacy documents, such as air waybills, whereas the new semantic models needed to follow the digital twin concept. Digital twinning—the mapping of a physical asset to a digital platform, provides a one-to-one mapping of real objects or concepts such as containers, flights, bookings and itineraries. The work was highly iterative, but the resulting digital twinning approach significantly facilitates interoperability with other transport modes. It does not matter what the modal differences are, freight is freight, a container is a container, a port is a port, and so on. We can argue about the models themselves, but we cannot argue about the things they represent.

The API and security infrastructure presented an interesting challenge. Almost all design patterns around APIs and security assume that there is a central system to which a client needs access. For example, if a client needs weather maps, they sign up to a weather service, obtain a digital key and access the data as needed via an API. The ONE Record data sharing concept is sometimes referred to as the Internet of Logistics, and just like the Internet, it assumes that parties are equal in the exchange. There are no natural digital service providers. When a forwarder needs a schedule update from a carrier for the purpose of making a booking, the roles of provider and clients are interchanged as the process evolves. This meant that the ONE Record API and security specification had to support that flexible relationship without the availability of a central authority to manage these relationships and exchanges. This platform interchange pattern exists between financial institutions, but it is not common elsewhere.

Much of the development and learning has been supported by technical pilot tests and by hackathons. IATA developed an open software 'ONE Record sandbox' that allowed anyone to deploy the infrastructure or use a common platform already set up to test all the aspects of the specification. Such tools provided valuable test input and allowed the community to incrementally propose, develop, test, and validate the ONE Record specifications.

Development of standards like ONE Record required many decisions, and the cooperation of a small but representative group of experts and stakeholders made this possible. Such an environment is readily available in industry-based organisations like IATA and the DCSA which represent the bulk of their carrier members and have the resources and commitment to see projects like this through. It is less certain that the relevant intergovernmental entities would have the authority to be business focused enough to make and enforce design and business choices on behalf of their constituents. Neither is it clear that they would have the willingness or authority to maintain such digitalisation standards once they have been developed.

10   The Proven Benefits of Digital Transformation

As IATA has shown, the shift to digitalisation is well worth the effort. IATA's biggest impact in digitalisation is in passenger transport. When IATA developed e-ticketing and stopped printing paper ticket stock in 2008, it reduced the industry ticket management cost by an estimated USD 3 billion by avoiding the need for printing, global distribution, collection and processing of tickets and boarding passes. The introduction of self-printable baggage tags, smartphone boarding passes, and self-service terminals has provided similar cost reductions, but more importantly, it changed the customer travel experience forever. It is now common practice to plan and execute air travel on a single digital platform—your mobile phone.

The impact of digitalisation on airfreight is harder to quantify since almost all freight has some documents that still need to be in paper format. Typically, these are certificates and documents associated with the freight rather than the transport itself. It is estimated that paper airwaybills incur an expense of USD10. The global cost savings from using an e-Air Waybills (e-AWB) would be over USD100 million per year. Increasingly, customs in the largest markets are enforcing the use of electronic documents for advanced cargo information. This allows them to undertake risk assessment in advance and pre-clear goods.

Not only in the airline industry, but in banking, telco, entertainment, retail and media, digital standards have been creating value for some time. As a result, these industries have also produced a better customer experience and a higher degree of efficiency and innovation. The DCSA strongly believes that container shipping can achieve similar results.

Compare the Electronic Bill of Lading (eBL) and the e-Air Waybill for freight in the airline industry. In 2010, IATA introduced e-AWB for airfreight. In November 2020, adoption of e-AWB was at 74% and is forecast to be 100% by the end of 2022. In December 2020, DCSA released its first set of eBL standards. If the container shipping industry starts adopting eBL standards in earnest, DCSA projects that a 50% adoption rate is feasible by 2030. At 50% adoption, it is estimated that the industry can potentially save more than USD4 billion per year, considering a global economic growth rate of 2.4% through 2030, as forecast by the OECD (2021).

While tech giants and various intergovernmental organisations are encouraging digitalisation in the container industry, no one knows what needs to be done to transform the industry (or how it can best be done) as well as the industry itself. As an industry-based non-profit organisation founded by some of the industry's foremost players and staffed with executives who have decades of industry experience, the DCSA therefore considers that it is uniquely positioned to speed container shipping's transition into the digital age.

The DCSA's deep connection to the container shipping industry combined with the collaborative and open way in which its standards are developed has garnered interest from many prominent stakeholders, and carrier members have committed to implementing the standards as part of their digitalisation strategies. As a result of this collaboration, DCSA has already established standards in a number of key areas including: Track & Trace, Internet of Things (IoT), Operational Vessel Schedules, Just-in-Time Port Call, eBL (as the first step towards eDocumentation) and Cyber-security. The standards are open and available for anyone (DCSA 2021e) to use to ensure widespread adoption can be achieved as rapidly as possible.

11   Closing Rermarks

As highlighted by the COVID-19 pandemic, the need to replace antiquated shipping processes with efficient, digital processes is more urgent than ever. A standardised, scaleable approach is the only way to future-proof such a fragmented, complex, and global industry. Collaboration among industry stakeholders is crucial to transforming the industry. DCSA is actively seeking involvement and input from all relevant stakeholders.

The aim of digital standards is greater transparency, which will foster a higher level of trust between stakeholders. Once trust through transparency is established, real innovation can occur—innovation that will enable reliable, easy to use, secure and environmentally friendly container transportation services.

The DCSA provides regular updates on its progress at: www.dcsa.org. Interested parties can also make contact and engage with the DCSA via the same website.

References

Apache (2021) Community-led development "The Apache way". Apache license version 2.0. The Apache Software Foundation. https://www.apache.org/licenses/LICENSE-2.0. Accessed 4 Feb 2021

Becha H, Schroeder M, Voorspuij J, Frazier T, Lind M (2021) Global data exchange standards: the basis for future smart container digital services. In: Lind M, Michaelides M, Ward R, Watson RT (eds) Maritime informatics. Springer, Heidelberg

Cauwer ND, Fontanet M, Abril J, Greven JT, Juhl JS, Probert S, Renz M, Rødseth ØJ (2021) The IMO reference data model—one solution fits most! In: Lind M, Michaelides M, Ward R, Watson RT (eds) Maritime informatics: additional perspectives and applications. Springer, Heidelberg

DCSA (2021a) Data and interfaces. The Digital Container Shipping Association (DCSA). https://dcsa.org/initiatives/data-and-interfaces. Accessed 4 Feb 2021

DCSA (2021b) Industry blueprint. The Digital Container Shipping Association (DCSA). https://dcsa.org/initiatives/industry-blueprint. Accessed 4 Feb 2021

DCSA (2021c) DCSA OpenAPI specification for Track & Trace. The Digital Container Shipping Association (DCSA). https://app.swaggerhub.com/apis/dcsaorg/DCSA_TNT/2.0.0. Accessed 4 Feb 2021

DCSA (2021d) DCSA—OpenAPI. The Digital Container Shipping Association (DCSA). https://github.com/dcsaorg/DCSA-OpenAPI. Accessed 4 Feb 2021

DCSA (2021e) Standardisation initiatives. The Digital Container Shipping Association (DCSA). https://dcsa.org/initiatives. Accessed 4 Feb 2021

IATA (2021) ONE record—one step closer to digital cargo, IATA. https://www.iata.org/en/programs/cargo/e/one-record/. Accessed 4 Feb 2021

ICS (2014) Shipping, world trade and the reduction of CO2 emissions: United Nations Framework Convention on Climate Change (UNFCCC), The International Chamber of Shipping (ICS)

JCP (2021) Java Community Process: JCP procedures overview. Java Community Process (JCP). https://www.jcp.org/en/procedures/overview. Accessed 4 Feb 2021

OECD (2021) OECD economic outlook: statistics and projections. OECD. https://www.oecd-ilibrary.org/economics/data/oecd-economic-outlook-statistics-and-projections_eo-data-en. Accessed 4 Feb 2021

Postman (2021) Postman API client. Postman. https://www.postman.com/product/api-client/. Accessed 4 Feb 2021

Sea-Intelligence (2019) SeaIntel maritime analysis, Global Liner report July 2019 as summarized by Verband der Chemischen Industrie (VCI)

UNECE (2021) Reference Data Models (RDM), UNECE. https://unece.org/trade/uncefact/rdm. Accessed 4 Feb 2021

Watson RT, Lind M, Delmeire N, Liesa F (2021) Shipping: a self-organising ecosystem. In: Lind M, Michaelides M, Ward R, Watson RT (eds) Maritime informatics. Springer, Heidelberg

Boosting the Effectiveness of Containerised Supply Chains: A Case Study of TradeLens

Jonas Louw-Reimer ⓘ, Jacob Liocouras Müller Nielsen ⓘ,
Niels Bjørn-Andersen ⓘ, and Norbert Kouwenhoven ⓘ

1 Introduction

The invention and introduction of containers in international trade in the 1950s was one of the most important innovations fuelling the growth in globalisation and international trade (Watson et al. 2017). To a varying degree, this enabled individual actors to achieve substantial operational efficiency. However, only very recently, the industry has focussed on the effectiveness and optimisation of the overall inter-organisational systems, where the use of information systems enabled substantially larger effectiveness gains.

Today, the containerised maritime transport industry is still overwhelmingly based on manual paper-based processes. This results in significant administrative costs, high inefficiencies, low sustainability, and the risk of fraud. In a largely paper-based and scattered network of systems, it can be difficult to verify the validity and authenticity of documents, as independent systems, and actors intentionally or unintentionally can tamper with information and cause errors along the supply chains.

J. Louw-Reimer
Copenhagen Business School, Copenhagen, Denmark
e-mail: jolo16ac@student.cbs.dk

J. L. M. Nielsen
Copenhagen Business School, Frederiksberg, Denmark
e-mail: jani16af@student.cbs.dk

N. Bjørn-Andersen (✉)
Department of Digitalization, Copenhagen Business School, Frederiksberg, Denmark
e-mail: nba@cbs.dk

N. Kouwenhoven
IBM NL, Amsterdam, The Netherlands
e-mail: Norbert.Kouwenhoven@nl.ibm.com

© The Author(s), under exclusive license to Springer Nature Switzerland AG 2021   95
M. Lind et al. (eds.), *Maritime Informatics*, Progress in IS,
https://doi.org/10.1007/978-3-030-72785-7_6

Accordingly, the most recent development in maritime informatics is the collection and sharing of information along the supply chains using digital platforms, which have the capacity to enable a thriving ecosystem for effective containerised global transportation by facilitating information sharing and horizontal information communities in a standardised digital form.

It is useful to think of this as a digitalised maritime self-organised ecosystem, which consists of the software platforms, all independent actors in the container trade, and software developers. The participation of the latter enables the development of extended functionality on the digital platforms and the integration with the information systems of participating actors. Together this spurs ecosystem co-creation of new and innovative service offerings based on the data available on the platforms.

Digital data sharing platforms have the capacity to orchestrate a digitalised network of interconnected trade actors. The facilitation of data sharing and collaboration enables true information sharing in near real-time based on trusted transactions. Well-managed platforms can work as a catalyst for ecosystem innovation and co-creation of new digital offerings bringing substantial benefits to all parties.

Today we see the emergence of several initiatives to enable digitally sharing of data across the different organisations in the maritime ecosystem. The Global Shipping Business Network (GSBN), the Digital Transport and Logistics Forum (DTLF) concept of a federative platform, INTTRA, and the World Economic Forum platform for Trade and Global Economic Interdependence are other examples of digital data sharing platforms in maritime supply chains. These platforms share the objective of ensuring efficient supply chains through the use of digital data sharing among their members. Given the various different systems on offer, interoperability between these different platforms is important to achieve their common goal of full supply chain visibility.

In order to provide a more detailed understanding of the functionality, advantages, and challenges of such platforms, we analyse the TradeLens platform. This is a digital industry platform jointly developed by IBM and GTD Solution Inc., a software company owned by A.P. Møller Maersk. In January 2018, IBM and Maersk announced their intention to build a digital platform for the shipping industry. In August 2018, the TradeLens beta product was formally launched, and in December of the same year, its general availability was announced. Five of the six largest cargo liner companies announced their intention to join the platform in July 2019 extending the scope of the platform to more than half of the world's ocean container cargo (TradeLens 2019c). In a recent press release of TradeLens (October 2020), it was stated that: *"the TradeLens ecosystem now includes more than 175 organizations—extending to more than 10 ocean carriers and encompassing data from more than 600 ports and terminals. Already it has tracked 30 million container shipments, 1.5 billion events and roughly 13 million published documents"* (TradeLens 2020c).

The vision behind the TradeLens platform is to build: *"greater trust, transparency, and collaboration across supply chains to help promote global trade"* (TradeLens 2019a). The TradeLens platform aims to liberate parties involved in trade from legacy data systems, manual document handling, and the current lack of transparency in supply chains. The TradeLens platform was created with four distinct objectives in mind:

- Connecting all the ecosystem's actors;
- Fostering collaboration and trust;
- Driving true information sharing;
- Spurring innovation.

In this chapter, we elaborate on the elements of the digitalised maritime ecosystem using the TradeLens platform as a case study.

2 Digitalisation of the Maritime Ecosystem for Container Traffic

The maritime ecosystem consists of a large number of independent actors each with different objectives and requirements. However, they are dependent on the actions of others for their effective operations (Lind et al. 2020, 2021). To achieve end-to-end supply chain visibility, it is necessary to facilitate effective digital data sharing and collaboration among all actors. The intention of the different platform initiatives is to do just that.

According to its home page, the TradeLens platform supports the global maritime container-based supply-chain, including ports and terminals, ocean carriers, customs and government authorities, intermodal operators, shippers, and beneficial cargo owners, freight forwarders, and financial services providers (Minarovits 2018). Furthermore, it is described as an "open and neutral supply chain platform underpinned by blockchain technology, enabling information sharing and collaboration across supply chains, thereby increasing industry innovation, reducing trade friction and ultimately promoting more global trade".

In order to provide a better understanding of the role of TradeLens in the complex network of interrelated actors, we will explore each of the actors below.

2.1 Ports and Terminals

Ports and terminals support trade by providing up-to-date information on all shipments within their boundaries. Ports and terminals handle an increasingly complex community of interrelated actors including the large land-based community (trucking traffic in metro areas, increased use of rail to move containers, and different inland depot locations to avoid congestion). Both the maritime and the land-based supply-chains need to be in synchronisation, and as a result, they all rely heavily on transparent communication and tight collaboration. The platform is intended to substantially assist ports and terminals in enriching their ability to deliver better value to their customers and increase their competitive potential (Minarovits 2018).

2.2   Ocean Carriers

More than 90% of global trade travels by ocean carriers. To handle the complex information processing for an ocean carrier with up to 20,000 containers, a high level of digitalisation is required to enable efficient data sharing, the automation of repetitive tasks, and near real-time container tracking during transport. Ocean carriers can help other actors by providing information regarding the disposition of shipments during their time at sea. The TradeLens platform addresses this by reducing manual customer service through increased transparency and reducing integration costs through the use of standardised application programming interfaces (APIs) (Minarovits 2018).

2.3   Customs and Government Authorities

Customs and government authorities ensure the legitimacy of exported and imported goods. This includes information regarding the clearance status for shipments in and out of a country. Currently, this entails a great deal of manual paperwork and information sharing across multiple authorities and agencies. The TradeLens platform enables authorities to make more informed risk assessments, provides increased transparency in information sharing, and enables collaboration across borders and countries through a unified platform, helping them control and facilitate trade in the supply chain (Minarovits 2018).

2.4   Intermodal Operators

Intermodal operators handle transport between shippers, warehouses, and ports/terminals. They provide information on the status and whereabouts of shipments carried by trucks, rail, barges, etc. Their main job is to ensure clear visibility and secure document handling, enabling them to make informed decisions increasing the efficiency of asset planning, and improving the service offerings to their customers. The TradeLens platform aims to provide all the right documents, at the right time in a secure and reliable way, helping intermodal operators take intelligent informed decisions and optimise asset planning (Minarovits 2018).

2.5 Shippers and Beneficial Cargo Owners (BCO)

Shippers and BCOs are the exporters and importers that manage the shipment before it is shipped, and after it has arrived at its destination. Their main role is to engage with the platform, as a consumer of the available information, to streamline their logistics and increase the efficiency of clearance processes. For these actors, the TradeLens platform should provide reliable end-to-end visibility across all parties and individual shipments, enhancing collaboration with freight forwarders and improving customer experience and satisfaction (Minarovits 2018).

2.6 Freight Forwarders/3PL

Freight forwarders handle everything from booking, arranging, transportation, and delivery of goods to the consumer. Traditionally, several manual processes and paper-based document processes resulted in low efficiency and lacklustre customer experiences. To support the freight forwarders in solving these challenges, the TradeLens platform provides them with access to near real-time information across the supply chain. This allows freight forwarders to greatly improve efficiency, improve track-and-trace tools, securely and reliably share documents and decrease handling costs, by automating manual electronic data exchange (EDI) entries, while increasing trust with partners, through transparent information flows and interconnectivity (Minarovits 2018).

2.7 Financial Services Providers

Financial services providers handle the massive number of transactions which occur every day in global trade. Many transactions in the industry are enabled by extending credit or other forms of guarantees from financial services providers. Hitherto, the lack of transparency in trade made many financial transactions involving risk assessment exceedingly difficult. This resulted in decreased scalability and accessibility to capital for a large portion of actors in the global economy. The TradeLens platform seeks to make risk assessment much easier (Minarovits 2018).

2.8 Document Sharing Among the Ecosystem Actors

Responding to the maritime informatics concerns of data sharing and digital collaboration across the self-organised ecosystem of maritime and global supply chains, all platforms need to have strict and transparent 'rules' for data sharing. Managing access permissions and data provision requirements about events and documents is a key activity in the TradeLens platform. This functionality is deeply integrated within its architecture. Documents uploaded to the platform are automatically associated with one of the following three trade objects, according to their type, in line with the UN/CEFACT standards:

- Shipment (the trade of goods);
- Consignment (the transportation of goods);
- Transport equipment (e.g., containers).

A trade document, for example, a commercial invoice, relates to the shipment whereas a transport document, such as a bill of lading, relates to the consignment. Thus, the documents originate from various participants in the ecosystem depending on the type of document. For instance, trade documents are uploaded by the shippers, whereas transport documents are uploaded by the transport service providers (IBM Corporation and GTD Solution Inc. 2020).

Actors upload the various document types to the platform as either structured JavaScript Object Notation (JSON) or unstructured documents (PDF, JPG, etc.). If available, documents uploaded in a structured format allow for automated re-use of the same information for the creation of other documents, such as the import declaration. Once uploaded at the origin, all permissioned participants can access the documents, including government authorities, such as customs.

In other words, the 'data sharing specifications' for the TradeLens platform, that every participant signs up to, precisely specify with whom and for what object type certain data is shared. For example, the truck driver moving the container sees fewer data elements than the BCO. The information and communication technology (ICT) setup (including strong encryption) protects the data-sharing model from tampering and spoofing. Specifically, data sharing 'rules' in the documentation of the platform are referred to as the 'Data Sharing Specifications'. These specifications are carried out using 'channels' and assigning each actor with 'roles' while the system is protected with strong encryption.

For a conceptual picture of the key actors and key data exchanged on the TradeLens platform, see Fig. 1.

3 Technical Overview of the TradeLens Platform

3.1 Hybrid Cloud

The TradeLens platform is built, deployed, and hosted on the IBM Hybrid Cloud platform, where the "hybrid cloud confines and unifies public and private cloud services from multiple could vendors to create a single, flexible, cost-optimal IT infrastructure" (Vennam 2019). This is a full-stack platform combining and unifying various public and private cloud services from both internal and external cloud vendors used by the actors of the TradeLens platform. The hybrid cloud caters for

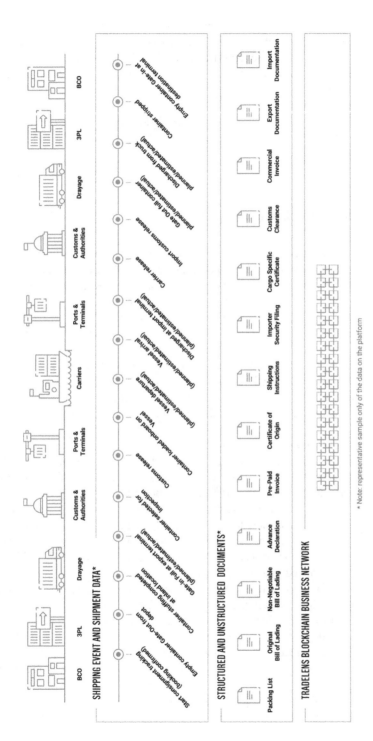

Fig. 1 Data sharing concept (TradeLens 2020a)

an organisation's data residency requirements; that is, to have specific types of data processed in on-premises data centres or in private clouds (IBM 2020). So, the TradeLens platform can be deployed simultaneously in both platform actors' private clouds without the restrictions of network bandwidth, security exposures, and legal requirements, and in the public cloud services whereby resources are being dynamically provisioned over the internet by third party providers (Anthonopoulos and Gillam 2017). This enables actors to join the platform without giving up control of their business-critical data while still benefitting from the flexibility of a public cloud where applicable (Vennam 2019).

3.2 Permissioned Blockchain

Ensuring trust with data sharing on the TradeLens platform is addressed using permissioned blockchain technology powered by the IBM Blockchain platform, which is deployed on the IBM Hybrid Cloud, and based on the Hyperledger Fabric, an open source blockchain framework for business networks.

Blockchain technology is a new type of shared database or ledger. A blockchain is a distributed peer-to-peer database with no central authority and no single point of trust. Instead, blockchain enables several actors to maintain and update the database. The consensus protocol ensures that only if all decentralised databases are identical, is a given transaction accepted. In this way, blockchain technology facilitates a shared trust among actors. In other words, the actors on the blockchain validate the information published to it and thus eliminate the need for a third party to control the data.

Shared databases in environments with limited trust or conflicting interests, such as sensitive document sharing in the maritime industry, give rise to several concerns for organisations. These include whom to trust with your shared data, how to identify persons or organisations involved in data sharing, what people or organisations can do to the database, etc. Blockchain technology helps overcome these problems.

The fact that the blockchain technology used on the TradeLens platform is permissioned means that actors are known to the network and that those actors need to meet certain requirements to gain access to and perform certain activities on the blockchain (Hyperledger.org 2018). The permissioned structure ensures that only permissioned parties can see specific types of information related to a trade object. The platform assigns rights according to the actors role in the ecosystem and the data type, following a unified permission matrix (TradeLens 2020b). Each node hosts the blockchain platform components and dedicated blockchain-managed document storage for that node. The TradeLens platform and each ocean carrier on the platform can host and manage a node, which comprises the infrastructure of the blockchain. Thus, the distributed ledger creates the 'peer to peer' model, where none of the carriers 'owns' a centralised database. Documents are stored only on a single node and are segregated by channels that enable the sharing of documents with only specific parties, thereby protecting members against information disclosure to third parties, such as competing cargo liners. In principle, a channel is established for each ocean carrier on the platform, although the current implementation is such that a few carriers do not have their own channel. Blockchain is used alongside object storage, document databases, and relational databases on the platform depending on the type of information and data sharing requirements (IBM Corporation and GTD Solution Inc. 2019).

Blockchain-technology ensures that transactions recorded on the chain are extremely hard to change without every node agreeing. In settings where trust is not an issue, it might not be necessary to have this immutable log of transactions. Accordingly, for documents in trade that are not subject to limited trust and already shared today as structured or unstructured documents, it is better to store these in relational databases to achieve better performance and lower cost. TradeLens has incorporated this by providing blockchain security for selected document types, and for the rest of the documents, traditional relational databases has been provided either on-premises or in the cloud.

3.3   Global Data Exchange Standards

"Standards will ensure the Shipping Information Pipelines integrates seamlessly in a way similar to how the Internet works today" (Jensen and Yao-Hua 2015). In line with this principle, the TradeLens platform incorporates the Supply Chain Reference Data Model (SCRDM) of the United Nations Centre for Trade Facilitation and Electronic Business (UN/CEFACT) to ensure easy and standardised interchange and interoperability of information models and digital encoding between the TradeLens platform and the various domains within the supply chain (TradeLens 2020b). Data on the TradeLens platform is organised and shared following the trade objects defined by the UN/CEFACT SCRDM: Shipments, Consignments, and Transport Equipment. Data published to the platform is assigned to one of these three standard trade objects (TradeLens 2020a).

Furthermore, TradeLens incorporates other standards such as ISO 6346 for container types, the United Nations Code for Trade and Transport Locations (UN/LOCODE) and Ship Message Design Group (SMDG) codes for locations, and ISO8601 for date/time format. The platform is also aligned with the track and trace and bill of lading standards recently published by the Digital Container Shipping Association (DCSA), a forum of the world's largest ocean carriers to align on information technology standards (DCSA 2021).

The Standard Business Exchange Structures of UN/CEFACT (the semantic standardisation) are implemented on the TradeLens platform to ensure platform neutrality and availability of the platform to any party of a shipment, anywhere in the world. Standards ensure that the data model supports the business and regulatory processes involved in the supply chain across borders (UN/CEFACT 2017). The digital encoding of the semantic standards also follows a second set of standards known as technical standards. The TradeLens platform is based on the JSON standard. Since the data exchange language of many carriers and other actors in the ecosystem is based on Extensible Mark-up Language (XML), the platform also provides conversions.

In this way, TradeLens has attempted to make sure that the various technical standards applied in the industry result in consistent, correct communication of data sets across the same theme between the different parties (Lind et al. 2020, 2021).

3.4   Security Considerations

Sensitive documents and data are saved and stored on the blockchain network of the TradeLens platform, where the permissioned blockchain ensures the immutability and traceability of documents. Furthermore, the data are protected with encryption technology. The cryptographic identification of every user and organisation protects against spoofing. The solution is protected under comprehensive security and the platform is accredited with ISO27K certifications (Biazetti 2019).

3.5   Architecture Overview

As mentioned earlier, the TradeLens ecosystem consists of actors connected to or providing data to the platform, the platform itself, and a set of applications and services presented in a marketplace atop the platform. Technically, the platform service layer consists of the services and functionality organised in micro services, which are linked using a publish/subscribe service.

The APIs of the platform connect the actors to the platform and allow for integration of in-house systems via non-proprietary, publicly available APIs, enabling near real-time data transfer via publish, subscribe, query, and document sharing functions. The APIs can reduce the cost of EDI maintenance and operation for ecosystem actors. The platform APIs deliver functionality directly to the actors and allow carriers to publish data to the platform. Where it is not possible for an actor to connect using an API, a connection can be established via the TradeLens Integration Framework, which is a component to facilitate the connection to the TradeLens APIs for organisations that are not API capable.

3.6   TradeLens Marketplace

The TradeLens marketplace provides several TradeLens applications including, the TradeLens Core, the TradeLens Electronic Bill of Lading (eBL), and third-party applications. The marketplace enables third party software developers to leverage ecosystem data to build value creating applications for the ecosystem (TradeLens 2019b). The TradeLens Core application creates a unified platform for sharing information, events, and documents, which allows actors to reduce the number of paper-based processes. The TradeLens eBL is an end-to-end solution that digitises the issuance, transfer, and surrender of original bills of lading, in a secure and streamlined manner (TradeLens 2020b).

3.7 TradeLens Core

The TradeLens Core is intended to be an end-to-end digital freight-management tool, ensuring full visibility and collaboration across the supply chain within the maritime industry. This includes tools for:

- Gaining transport insights;
- Managing shipments;
- Sharing documents;
- Visualising dashboards;
- Receiving near real-time notifications;
- Controlling partner access;
- Integrating with publicly available APIs;
- Utilising data to develop and improve performance and offerings.

These core tools in the TradeLens Core provide key network actors with near real-time end-to-end visibility, which at any point in time allow them to manage shipments across the supply chain. The advanced access control also allows actors to provide their partners with precisely the information they need in near real-time. In other words, the TradeLens Core seeks to ensure the authenticity of relevant documents through blockchain technology, minimising the risk of fraud, document tampering, and errors. This should result in reduced costs and accelerated workflows across the supply chain (TradeLens 2019b).

3.8 TradeLens Electronic Bill of Lading (eBL)

The eBL (compared to the physical BL) attempts to reduce the costs of one of the costliest and most time-consuming processes in the supply chain, namely the issuing, transferring, and surrendering of the paper-based original bills of lading. The BL itself entitles the holder to the goods shipped, and anyone who can provide this document is entitled to have the cargo released. Accordingly, the process of an eBL needs to be highly secure, and it has to eliminate the risk of tampering, interception, forgery, etc.

The underlying encryption and permission blockchain technology allow for the proper digitisation of a document and the related processes. Accordingly, instead of issuing physical paper-based documents, the eBL provides an instrument for paperless handling. This helps reduce time and costs when it comes to handling the original bills of lading. Furthermore, digitising the bill of lading allows for increased security and transparency in terms of eliminating the risk of document loss, reducing delays due to physical transportation of documents, and eliminating the need for real-time versioning. In the full process, it is possible to track the documents via Hyperledgers in the blockchain. Accordingly, the eBL enables a standardised process, which provides cargo owners, freight forwarders, and shippers with a streamlined and uniform way of transferring and surrendering a bill of lading. "The eBL ensures a secure, legal and cost-efficient way of handling a previously very time-consuming, costly, and manual paper-based process" (TradeLens 2019b).

4   Benefits of Digital Data Sharing Platforms for the Full Supply Chain

Digitalising the global maritime supply chain is no easy task. The supply chain is complex, involving hundreds of actors, thousands of processes, and millions of documents. This obviously creates several challenges, many of which can be solved by digitalising the sharing of data and enabling seamless data exchange among ecosystem members (Pico 2019). Below we summarise the four benefits for the full supply chain.

Standardised Processes The first benefit relates to the lack of standardised technologies and processes, resulting in slow and inefficient information sharing and collaboration across the maritime supply chain (Becha et al. 2020). The TradeLens platform addresses this problem by providing standardised interfaces, such as the TradeLens Core and eBL, underpinned by blockchain. This enables the actors to share information in a secure way, which enhances their ability to track orders across multiple touchpoints and optimise applications and processes. Through standardised API integrations, the platform streamlines the supply chains and enables cross-organisational digitalised workflows (Minarovits 2018).

Visibility and Transparency The second benefit is in addressing the challenge of a lack of end-to-end visibility and transparency across the supply chain. Documents are often stored in multiple systems, in different formats (some digital, others paper-based), creating a complex network of interrelated entities (Pico 2019). For almost all actors, but especially for ports and terminals, it is valuable that the TradeLens platform provides end-to-end visibility and information across shipping corridors and delivers near real-time information, allowing ports and terminals to receive accurate information in advance to enable them to effectively plan and respond to expected as well as unexpected events. The TradeLens platform provides the ability to perform digital asset planning, making the need for a huge amount of manual paperwork and slow processes obsolete, by removing the silo structure of transportation and connecting the ecosystem (TradeLens 2019b).

To reap the full benefits of a data-sharing platform such as TradeLens, all relevant data elements about a container voyage must be available on the platform. There will be a natural coverage of consignment data from all the transporters that are on the platform. However, the shipment information (purchase orders, packing lists, commercial invoices, etc.) requires BCOs to participate as well, which is not always the case, although, as illustrated in the example below, there are vast benefits for the BCOs.

Early in 2020, a Dutch trading company wanted to know exactly when to pick up its imports from the Port of Rotterdam. It also wanted to reduce the time spent on preparing and producing customs declarations. The company requested its overseas suppliers to share the commercial documents for the relevant containers' departure on the TradeLens platform. A small piece of software was then written to provide daily alerts on the arrival of containers at the port terminal and to generate an import declaration; first presented on screen 'to check' and then to be submitted with one click. The result was a 5-min action instead of 50 min per declaration (Boughner and McQueen 2020).

Today, the TradeLens platform provides full visibility: the whereabouts of the incoming and outgoing containers, the exact customs release moment, and their arrival at client destination. This functionality has been operational since August 2020.

Security of Processes The third benefit relates to ensuring security in processes, where the maritime industry faces challenges related to lack of trust, tampering with documents and delays. This is especially the case in the bill of lading process, where the lack of trust and the need for authenticity for years has required the sending of original physical documents back and forth between actors. This is a very time-consuming manual process with a high risk of errors, lack of transparency, and the risks of fraud and corruption (Kamal 2017). However, the TradeLens platform overcomes this by allowing shippers and cargo owners to share information in a secure way. This also enhances their ability to track orders across multiple touchpoints and optimise applications and processes through standardised API integrations.

Especially ocean carriers benefit from a lower risk of fraud through digital audit trails and end-to-end information regarding shipment events, enabled by the permissioned blockchain technology.

Security and data integrity also extend to the interface with government agencies, where border crossing and customs compliance is one of the big cost drivers in the maritime sector. Collecting data, picking the right version, preparing forms, submitting them on time in the proper format, conducting lengthy dialogue with authorities asking for additional data when there are discrepancies or data inconsistencies, etc. These are all issues to be overcome.

The TradeLens platform allows customs authorities to see all relevant data. Customs are able to access substantially more information compared to a traditional import declaration and they will receive it much earlier in the journey. The data related to a container's voyage is available in near real-time and is collected at the time of departure. Accordingly, the incoming port customs authorities can start conducting risk assessments at departure time, and can conduct checks whenever they see fit. This can result in proactively warning importers to fix data inconsistencies, identifying the absence of relevant licenses, spotting illegal activities early, preparing for inspections on arrival, and even applying 'clearance at sea' if appropriate. Ultimately, it allows for completely waiving the need for import declaration forms. The Union Customs Code (UCC) describes a model for 'Declaration by entry in the declarant's ledger'. This is a paradigm shift for customs procedures—from 'data possession' to 'data access'.

Better Risk and Financial Assessment The fourth benefit is the provision of near real-time and immutable sources of information for financial services providers. The platform provides permission-based access and complete document integrity and validity as well as full transaction visibility to documents segregated by the use of channels. This helps them assess risk immediately, and they can provide trade financing and insurance to their clients much more effectively. Accordingly, this provides a strong foundation for ensuring true scalability and ability to tap into local as well as global growth (Minarovits 2018).

5   Diffusion and Adoption of Digital Data Sharing Platforms in the Maritime Ecosystem

Given the benefits of digital data sharing platforms, a growing number of key actors are now supporting and joining such platforms. To understand why others have yet to join, it is necessary to consider the underlying business assumptions of the various actors.

In the case of TradeLens, the platform distinguishes between network members (net data providers) and paying customers (net data consumers). The first group, for instance ocean cargo liners, publish the bill of lading and various other transport documents to the platform. These actors typically both provide data to the platform and consume data. The second group, for example shippers and BCOs, primarily consume data from the platform provided by the network members and only provide a limited amount of data to the platform (Felix Van Gemmern, TradeLens).

The time required to achieve connectivity to the platform depends on the use case/ business model of each actor, and the system or sources of data to be connected to the platform. Generally, the TradeLens platform is a software-as-a-service (SaaS) product working off-the-shelf, which does not require any integration to be used. For stand-alone situations, the process of joining the platform can take as little as 24 h. After signing a contract, an account is created for the customer, the identity is verified for data provisioning, and finally, if necessary, end-users receive training. On the other hand, there will also be those who opt for a much more integrated solution. These actors will typically have more complex in-house systems using proprietary databases, ERP systems or legacy systems that need to be connected to the TradeLens platform to automatically exchange data. Connecting this second group of actors to the platform takes longer. The time needed to become fully operational depends on the scope of data being provided and the interoperability of the legacy systems involved (Felix Van Gemmern, TradeLens).

Lowering the barriers for joining a platform in general and automating the feed of data specifically are important in achieving general adoption in the ecosystem. Most actors choose to have their core information systems (Navis, SAP, etc.) provide and receive data to and from the TradeLens platform automatically through either APIs or EDIs. For example, a terminal operator could send a 'gate out' message to the TradeLens' API by their Navis system.

The volume of potentially useful source data held by companies is normally far too big to submit manually. The creation of suitable interfaces requires an initial effort, but this is actually 'business as usual' for many of the IT departments of the ecosystem actors.

For the data providers, the main actors feeding the platform data, such integration typically requires substantial work and modification of their information systems especially if the ecosystem actors' legacy systems are not well documented or for other reasons are hard to integrate with. In these situations, the onboarding can sometimes be tedious. For the data consumers that primarily just need to subscribe to certain data points relevant to their business, the efforts to establish connections is typically very low.

Technical capabilities of an actor can be an issue. Actually, "*very low technical advancement, but also very high technical advancement, can be an obstacle for engagements*" (Felix Van Gemmern, TradeLens Onboarding Manager Actors, 2020). Actors with low technical capabilities may operate their business without dedicated information systems for document handling or data processing, and they might find it hard to connect the platform data to existing business processes. At the other end of the spectrum, established actors with highly technically advanced systems might already be connected to their main supply chain partners as part of their existing systems landscape. One example of technically advanced actors are the customs authorities in developed economies that already have well-established, digitalised setups: "*Because customs authorities have the backing of legal regulations, companies need to provide the information in the way customs are already set-up to require. Accordingly, for some customs authorities, it is not very high on their agenda to modify their systems to fit TradeLens standards, since actors are obliged to provide information in a format that fits their system*" (Felix Van Gemmern, TradeLens).

While, as van Gemmern points out, there is no pressing obligation for customs authorities to change, some of the technically advanced customs authorities are interested in new and more effective ways of working by reducing the volume of transactions and declarations that they must risk-assess. Along the same lines, more efficient customs procedures are increasingly being recognised by governments as a means to facilitate trade, which can create a competitive edge for regions or states striving to attract economic activities.

The availability of data from a platform such as TradeLens empowers customs authorities to transform their mind-set: moving from a reactive scheme towards a more proactive scheme, where customs authorities can prepopulate declaration forms (de-risked as documents are sourced straight from the TradeLens platform) or even waive declarations for actors on the TradeLens platform. The transparency and immutability of such a platform guarantees an accurate picture, has the appropriate level of detail, and is available early. Accordingly, pilot implementations of the TradeLens platform within some customs authorities are in progress, and the need for any necessary legislative changes are now being explored.

So in summary, there is generally little resistance among most ecosystem actors: *"We do not see a lot of resistance to join the platform, in fact we are seeing the opposite, huge interest and lots of engagement"* (Felix Van Gemmern, TradeLens).

6 Future Challenges of Digital Data Sharing Platforms

In order to achieve the full benefit of a digital platform like TradeLens, there are a number of future challenges, which we shall discuss below.

A future challenge is the ownership and disclosure of data. As discussed previously, to reap the full benefits of data sharing platforms, all relevant data elements about a container voyage must be available on the platform. In the case of the TradeLens platform, there is currently (2021) a substantial difference between the availability of consignment data and shipment data. This is likely to be the same with other similar platforms.

With regard to consignment data, details of 99% of all consignments are available today in digital form since most transporters are network members of the TradeLens platform. This allows for fully automated creation and processing of all transport datasets/documents. This includes customs Entry/Exit documents and Cargo Manifest related procedures. Accordingly, Entry Summary Declarations (ENS) manifests and Arrival Notifications (AN) can all be generated directly from data available on the TradeLens platform.

On the other hand, the availability of shipment data is dependent upon the participation of sellers and buyers. For full load containers, where the shipper directly engages with the carriers, this is a perfect model. When the shipper uses intermediaries (third party logistics ((3PL)) to transport shipments, the 3PL is making the booking of the consignments on the TradeLens platform. The BCO must then allow or order the 3PL to provide the shipment data to the TradeLens platform. Unfortunately, some 3PL actors see the platform as a competitor, rather than as a partner, and they only want to share the consignment data.

However, to achieve optimisation and effectiveness in the more extended supply chain, all commercial shipment information (purchase order, packing list, commercial invoice, etc.) must be available on the platform. This requires the BCO (or the freight forwarder representing the BCO) to be participating. Unfortunately, this is not always the case since there is a certain amount of resistance on behalf of freight forwarders to allow 'their' information on the platform.

A second future challenge is not technical and is of a completely different nature: some existing aggregators/platforms feel threatened, especially where their business model is based on collecting information and reselling it. We can take the example of a port having a port community system (PCS), which aims to improve transparency, data sharing, and processes in a port. Clearly, this actor will want to have access to the data that the TradeLens platform can provide. Furthermore, it will be willing to share local details back to the TradeLens platform. However, where the business model of the PCS is to sell data and make money out of the otherwise lack of information at the port level, the TradeLens platform will be seen as a competitor, because it makes this information generally available. Thus, to maintain their current business model, these ports will try to bypass the TradeLens platform and collect the same data as the TradeLens platform makes available from other (often secondary) sources. In these situations, the port authorities or PCS owners must decide, which model is the best for their port and region in the long run.

In relation to the second challenge, there is also potential resistance from customs brokers, as declaration form filling—a source of income today—might soon be an obsolete task. When governments start providing prepopulated declaration forms, or even adopt a full waiving of declarations for actors on platforms such as the TradeLens platform, the same evolution looms as we have seen for income tax advisors, where the prepopulated income tax forms killed off much of the form filling business. Tax advisors had to change their business model and aim at higher value advice instead. Similarly, customs brokers will have to adapt their business models towards areas like supervising/certification of trade lanes, vouching for completeness of data provided to the data sharing platforms, validating the veracity of inputs, etc. A 'certified broker' could vouch for a trade lane and negotiate facilitation schemes, or they could make sure that supply chain data will be properly available, so that border authorities can access the data whenever they see fit, whether it is for targeting, levying duties or other reasons.

A third future challenge is that geopolitics plays a huge role in global supply chains. Even though the TradeLens platform is an open system and has by far the widest global coverage, some countries/regions want to have their own regional or even global network. They prefer their own technical solutions, their own encryption techniques, and their own platform governance models.

In November 2020, the Global Shipping Business Network (GSBN) was launched as a direct competitor to the TradeLens platform running on an Oracle hybrid cloud. GSBN participants include among others COSCO Shipping, COSCO Shipping Ports, Hutchison Ports, PSA International, Shanghai International Port, CMA CGM, and Hapag-Lloyd. Even though the initial list of members includes two of the largest European ocean liners, the overall composition suggests that this can be considered an Asian platform, where Asian ocean carriers are the orchestrators of the platform.

Although to some extent the TradeLens platform and GSBN appear to be competing, "*I sincerely doubt there will be only one platform in the future. There needs to be interoperability, and the way to [secure] that interoperability is to have standards. Where standards are in place, we'll embrace them. It's easier to connect to a host of carriers if they're agreeing on the same standards*" (Michael White, director TradeLens[1]). White is referring to a future, where there will be a network of networks, and where the logistic platforms from various regions will have to agree on data exchange standards, data privacy protection standards, etc. The TradeLens platform already has various data exchange agreements with local and geo/regional platforms as part of moving towards global coverage.

7 Digital Data Sharing Platforms as a Catalyst for Further Digital Innovation in Global Trade

Today TradeLens is by far the largest global digital data sharing platform in containerised global trade, but it is only a few years old, and nobody expects it to have found its final form. Accordingly, one of its objectives is to spur innovation, where the platform is intended to work as a catalyst for further digital innovation in global trade. Its open API environment enables ecosystem members and independent software vendors to leverage ecosystem data to innovate and optimise business processes for individual actors or for (larger parts of) the full network. There are two main arguments for this development.

First, the TradeLens platform has documented and made its APIs, their structure, data model and the logic behind the solutions publicly available online for anybody to access.

Second, since the platform data model has been developed following open standards and promoting interoperability, this enables ecosystem members to easily incorporate data from the platform into existing IT infrastructure. In this way, the TradeLens platform enables software developers to build custom integrations for all trade actors. The intention is to ensure streamlined information flow between actors' internal systems and the API enabled core of the platform. As has been described earlier, the use of open standards and the promotion of interoperability does not mean that everything is publicly available and freely exchanged. At some stage in any business, there is a time when innovation goes beyond standards and becomes commercial-in-confidence. This is where competition starts. However, to obtain the highest level of effectiveness and sustainability, as soon as innovations spread, it is time to agree on new standards.

Third, through the TradeLens Marketplace, software developers can develop and publish innovative applications for existing or new customer segments, potentially helping actors reach new customers and expand their service offerings. The open-source architecture and standardised APIs allow software developers to seamlessly capture and create value by expanding their own value proposition. At the same

---

[1]https://www.joc.com/technology/dual-blockchains-shipping-test-interoperability_20190712.html.

time, they help grow and expand the TradeLens ecosystem, by connecting with supply and logistics data networks.

Digital data sharing platforms have the capacity to enable and increase the value of complementing technologies to further increase the digital transformation of the maritime sector. Automating manual processes beyond the offerings of the core data sharing platform with APIs enables new software that can provide substantial cost savings for individual actors along the supply chain, such as by using robotics process automation (RPA). RPA can enable automated custom workflows leading to cost savings for that individual actor. Additionally, digital data sharing platforms enable actors to share data with their supply chain partners, and in combination with IoT enabled sensors, near real-time information can be generated automatically without human intervention. This can further increase supply chain visibility and eliminate the need for manual data input. The cloud-based technology also enables shippers to employ IoT devices on transport equipment to broadcast GPS-based locations of containers to their network of partners for real-time tracking and planning. Finally, the sharing and provision of additional data of higher quality among ecosystem members enables the use of big data analytics for improving the operations of actors in the maritime ecosystem.

Digital data sharing platforms encourage co-creation of new digital offerings, such as applications and third-party integrations based on supply chain data among a variety of different actors with vastly different needs and requirements in the complex trade environment. This means that, although digital data sharing platforms have the potential to augment value creation processes within the organisational boundaries of each actor, the most important influence comes from its potential to facilitate a mutual co-creation process among the ecosystem of actors and third parties. In other words, the platforms enable a reengineering of the overall global, containerised transport ecosystem towards achieving much higher efficiency, security, and sustainability.

8   Closing Remarks

The success of data sharing platforms is measured by the amount of data shared such as the number of container voyages, the number of times data gets accessed, as well as its ability to help increase predictability in transport. All of this contributes to decreasing delays, reducing errors, economising on resources, and saving time. For the general success of data sharing platforms, we believe that in the future, there will be parallel, competing platforms, and competing networks. These will be offering a range of value propositions and a range of user experiences. We expect that such a range of global and regional platforms will contribute to avoiding a single platform lock-in. Platforms should be able to co-exist and share common data exchange protocols to provide all supply chain participants with a 360° view, by combining data from various platforms. As an example, TradeLens has an agreement with an Asian regional platform to exchange data according to mutually agreed standards.

Furthermore, we expect platforms to adhere to federative agreements such as the European Commission DTLF initiative. Its concept of a federative platform has been developed addressing the issues of having multiple network platforms, each with their own 'lens' or agenda, and each with their unique data model and content scope, making data sharing extremely difficult. The recommendation is that for data sharing platforms to be successful, each of the platforms should adhere to collective data models, or at least be able to translate data from each other.

Data sharing platforms such as the TradeLens platform are highly dependent on the broad adoption of the platform among actors along the complete supply chain. The success of the platform in the eyes of each actor in the supply chain is dependent on the participation of the other actors with whom they deal. If all of one's supply chain partners have joined the platform, this actor will most likely perceive the platform as a success. Therefore, to make the platform attractive to many actors, the larger actors in trade lanes with high influence, such as the customs authorities or huge traders like Walmart, can be key in getting more actors to join the platform as they can ask their trade-partners to submit required documents through the platform. Subsequently, the platform will be more attractive for the paying members (net data consumers).

In this way, we expect that these networked, digital platforms for data sharing will pave the way for a much more effective and sustainable global containerised trade.

References

Anthonopoulos N, Gillam L (2017) Cloud computing—principles, systems and applications, vol 15 (1), 2nd edn. Springer, Cham

Becha H, Lind M, Simha A, Bottin F, Larsen SE (2020) Standardisation in container shipping is key to boosting economies of scale – importance of data collaboration between shipping lines, Smart Maritime Network, 2020-05-14. https://smartmaritimenetwork.com/wp-content/uploads/2020/05/Standardisation-andthe-importance-of-data-collaboration-between-shipping-lines.pdf

Biazetti A (2019) Security—5 key points about TradeLens platform security, pp 1–8

Boughner Z, McQueen K (2020) Where is my container, where is my cargo, and where is my coffee? https://www.tradelens.com/post/where-is-my-container-where-is-my-cargo-and-where-is-my-coffee. Accessed 15 Jan 2021

DCSA (2021) DCSA publishes standards for the bill of lading

Hyperledger.org (2018) Hyperledger white paper—an introduction to Hyperledger. https://doi.org/10.1016/bs.adcom.2020.08.016

IBM (2020) IBM blockchain platform—technical overview. May. https://www.ibm.com/blockchain/platform

IBM Corporation and GTD Solution Inc. (2019) Solution architecture—TradeLens documentation

IBM Corporation and GTD Solution Inc. (2020) Document sharing—TradeLens documentation. https://docs.tradelens.com/documents/document_sharing/

Jensen T, Yao-Hua T (2015) Key design properties for shipping information pipeline. Lecture Notes Comput Sci 9373:491–502. https://doi.org/10.1007/978-3-319-25013-7_40. Including Subseries Lecture Notes in Artificial Intelligence and Lecture Notes in Bioinformatics

Kamal A (2017) Traditionals bills of lading V. Electronic bills of ladings: pros and cons and the way forward. The IRES International Conference, 19–21 Mar. http://www.uct.ac.za/depts/shiplaw/muthow2.htm

Lind M, Simha A, Becha H (2020) Creating value for the transport buyer with digital data streams. The Maritime Executive. https://maritime-executive.com/editorials/creating-value-for-the-transport-buyer-with-digital-data-streams

Lind M, Michaelides M, Ward R, Watson RT (2021) Maritime informatics. Springer, Cham

Minarovits C (2018) TradeLens overview. IBM, p 400

Pico S (2019) Two major obstacles hold digitization back in shipping. ShippingWatch, pp 1–3

TradeLens (2019a) Major ocean carriers CMA CGM and MSC to join TradeLens blockchain-enabled digital shipping platform. https://www.maersk.com/news/articles/2019/05/28/cma-cgm-and-msc-to-join-tradelens-digital-shipping-platform

TradeLens (2019b) Solution brief, pp 1–11. https://www.tradelens.com/wp-content/uploads/2019/05/TradeLens-Solution-Brief_Edition-Two.pdf

TradeLens (2019c) TradeLens adds major ocean carriers Hapag-Lloyd and Ocean Network Express. https://www.tradelens.com/press-releases/hapag-lloyd-and-ocean-network-express

TradeLens (2020a) Data sharing specification—TradeLens documentation. https://docs.tradelens.com/reference/data_sharing_specification/

TradeLens (2020b) Platform. https://www.tradelens.com/platform

TradeLens (2020c) Press release—CMA CGM and MSC complete TradeLens integration and join as foundation carriers. https://www.tradelens.com/press-releases/cma-cgm-and-msc-complete-tradelens-integration-and-join-as-foundation-carriers

UN/CEFACT (2017) Supply chain reference data model, 1–17 Jan. https://unece.org/fileadmin/DAM/uncefact/RSM/RSM_SCRDM_v1.0.0.2.pdf

Vennam S (2019) Hybrid cloud. https://www.ibm.com/cloud/learn/hybrid-cloud?lnk=fle

Watson R, Lind M, Haraldson S (2017) Physical and digital innovation in shipping: seeding, standardizing, and sequencing. Proceedings of the 50th Hawaii International Conference on System Sciences (2017), July. https://doi.org/10.24251/hicss.2017.579

Index

CPSIA information can be obtained
at www.ICGtesting.com
Printed in the USA
LVHW051154100621
689812LV00002B/105